Highlights
of
My Life

Highlights of My Life

A Memoir

PAUL D. NEUWIRTH

Copyright © 2017 Paul D. Neuwirth

All rights reserved. No part of this book may be reproduced or transmitted in any form or by any means, electronic or mechanical, including photocopying, recording, or by any information storage and retrieval system, except in the case of brief quotations embodied in critical articles and reviews, without prior written permission of the publisher.

Printed in the United States of America

LCN: 2017951667

ISBN: 978-1-947368-09-5
Ebook ISBN: 978-1-947368-10-1

Cover Design: Sherry L. Brown
Interior Design: Ghislain Viau

For the current and future generations of my family.

And also for those I have known who have helped and guided me along this journey.

Contents

Introduction	1
Family Origins	4
Home On Walton Avenue	5
The Smell of Comfort	11
My Ear to the Radio	13
A Pinball Escapade	15
There is a Right Way and There Was a Wrong Way	17
Hot Dogs and Summer Nights	19
Bagels and Sunday Newspapers	21
Beginning a Certified Public Accountant (CPA) Career and Where It Led	25
Manny Saxe and Teaching	27
On Faith and Principles	30
Just One Semester	32
Mountain Climbing	34
My Journey in Marketing	44
A Tale of Two Cities	49
The Chinese Wall	54
A Domino Effect	56

Sometimes More than a Hired Hand	60
An Uncommon Man	63
A Man of the World	66
A Multi-Talented Man	69
Photographs	71
Adventures in Scuba Diving	75
Air Time	78
Religious Observations	81
Real Estate Ventures	84
The World's Fair	90
A Big Book Needs an Editor	93
Stamp Collecting Opens the World	95
Always Skating	98
Building Scooters	102
Goodbye Walton Avenue	103
More About Mom	105
The Games We Played	109
Revisiting Roots	116
A Lesson in Miss Troskin's Class	122
Mr. Solomon's Lesson	124
The Junior High Championship	126
Globetrotting	129
Moments in Time	137
A Fall and Its Aftermath	140
The Writing is Completed	142

Introduction

On reaching my eightieth birthday, my wife Delaney and I spent a delightful afternoon with son Stephen. Over coffee, I said that one of my life's regrets is that I can no longer talk to my deceased mother and father. I said that, although I am familiar with the broad brushstrokes of my grandparents' origins, my parents had spoken little of the details of their own early lives.

Stephen's eyes lit up and, with Nataly on the telephone, they gave me a wonderful gift—the opportunity to write this book of the highlights of my life. Their gift is a way for me to talk to my children, grandchildren, and those who follow so that they will know about my childhood and beyond. This book is intended to tell my story and to encourage others, including the generations I will never meet, to do the same.

My impressions and observations of events that touched me in a positive or negative way, as well as some memories of the everyday parts of my life, are documented here in one form or another. Sometimes the stories intertwine.

You'll notice right away that this book isn't organized by date. It's episodic—thematic rather than strictly chronological. It was a more stimulating exercise, and one that I think better illustrates my character and personality, to focus the book on pivotal events in my life and describe how they led me to where I am today.

This volume is a guide to my travels through that foreign country that is the past. It is primarily a book of recollections, and we know that sometimes memory can be faulty. Any errors of fact are solely mine, and for them, I apologize in advance.

Children are certainly highlights for any father, and my sons have been and continue to be essential features in my life. Sprinkled among the pages of this book are references to Richard, Jim, and Stephen. They are the sweetest icing on the cake of my life, and they have been from the days they were born, throughout their formative years, and into maturity.

Although each of the brothers is unique, all three have certain qualities in common. Without doubt, they are exceptionally smart, talented, and brilliantly accomplished. Also, each has demonstrated a full measure of courage. These are men of honor and integrity. I continue to be awed by these boys, now men.

This story would be incomplete if it did not include memories of Beatrice Kleinberg Neuwirth, now deceased, my first wife and the mother of our three boys. Each of our sons loved Bea and each continues to carry an enduring love for her.

Bea and I were married for 25 years. In the main, they were good years for both of us. When the time came on my part for a separation, it was traumatic for both of us, as well as for our children.

That Bea was a fine mother can be seen in the personalities, talents, and characters of the children we raised.

After the separation from Bea that led to divorce, I met Delaney, who later became my wife. I began with somewhat limited expectations about how our relationship would turn out and for how long. Delaney, the love of my life, and I lived together for 17 years and married on December 31, 1999. We have been together now for 34 years.

HIGHLIGHTS OF MY LIFE

The highlights of my two marriages are not included in this volume. Privacy between husband and wife precludes me from delving into those matters here.

Family Origins

In about 1898 or 1899, Yetta Barken and Wolf Kaufman, my maternal grandparents, each came to the United States from Russia. They were Jews escaping discrimination and persecution. They met in the U.S. Although just about penniless, they married. My mother, Annie, was the oldest of their four children.

My paternal grandparents, Pearl Berger Neuwirth and Sam Neuwirth, left the Austro-Hungarian Empire in the 1880s for a brighter future in America. Sam was a tailor who made a comfortable living crafting men's suits from bolts of cloth. Benjamin, my father, was the youngest of Pearl and Sam's six children.

Both sets of families settled on Manhattan's notoriously overcrowded Lower East Side. My father's family lived at 2 Avenue D, while my mother's family eventually moved to Brooklyn. My mother left school at age 16 to help support her family, but she kept in touch with her high school friends. In the summers, the girls spent their vacations in a rented house at Far Rockaway Beach. My father and his friends also vacationed at Far Rockaway Beach, and that's where Annie and Ben met. After a long courtship, they married in 1931.

My parents have been gone for a while now. They enjoyed long, productive lives. Mom lived to be 97, and Dad to 102.

Home On Walton Avenue

I was born during a hot New York City summer on July 12, 1936. My family lived in a two-bedroom apartment on Walton Avenue, one block west of the Grand Concourse, in a section of the Bronx known today as the Grand Concourse Historic District. Back in those days, block after block of my neighborhood and those around it were lined with practically identical, six-story apartment buildings. Almost all of the apartments were rentals.

Every two years, as rental leases expired, many families moved from one building to another. The *en masse* relocations stopped in 1941 with World War II on the horizon. No new buildings went up. Rent control regulations removed incentives for new construction. Most everyone stayed where they were after that, including my family.

I don't remember much before the age of four, the year my sister Sylvia was born. It was 1940, and in those days, many parents feared that older children could infect newborns with incurable diseases. When my sister was brought home from the hospital and adults came to visit her and my mother, I was sent to another part of the apartment, alone. My mother would shut herself and the baby in her room, without me. I felt terribly excluded. I wasn't old enough yet to understand the rationale behind the separation. If I were to describe the feeling now, it would be a sense of abandonment. That early memory likely shaped some of my future actions, but who knows?

From the age of eight or nine, I spent a lot of time with my friends, and those friendships dominated my childhood.

Most of my friends lived on the same street as I did. Lining both sides of Walton Avenue between 164th and 165th Streets were five apartment houses, a synagogue, and a Catholic parochial school. My friends and I believed that spit of asphalt and concrete belonged to us. We played games that changed with the seasons: stickball, skelly (sliding bottle caps across a chalk diagram), and ringolevio (a kind of urban hide-and-seek that stretched across city blocks). Nobody plays these games anymore. On weekdays, after school, and almost all weekends, my friends and I roamed Walton Avenue, the neighboring streets, the parks, and the playground. We were basically without adult supervision until suppertime.

We never called each other by telephone to confirm who would be outside; our parents never organized "play dates." We just knew what games we wanted to play, and we organized ourselves. The neighborhood had large parks and playgrounds, and we felt safe there. However, if we left our neighborhood, we knew we were on other kids' turf; though we didn't feel threatened, we had our guard up. That said, safety didn't dominate our thoughts at all. Our games were rough, raucous, and immensely fun. They were powerful formative experiences for me.

When we were about ten or eleven, my friends and I formed a social athletic club, as many young boys did in neighborhoods around the city. These groups were the Aces, the Stars, the Spartans, and so on. Each club's members were from specific city blocks. Forming an athletic team was as much about playing sports as it was about representing home turf. We spent hours debating the right name for our club. Some of my friends had siblings three or five years older; they were the big kids, and we felt small next to them. So a natural choice for our team name was the *Midgets*.

No team was complete without "official" clothing, so we raised money—most of it from our parents—to buy club jackets. They were woolen on one side and satin on the reverse. "Midgets" was spelled out on each side, together with our own name and player number embroidered on the front and on the sleeves. As we grew, we purchased new, larger jackets. I wore mine with pride, as did all the kids. Although it is frayed and torn now, my Midgets jacket still hangs in my closet, and it fits me as well as it did when I was 16. Some of the rips and gashes were made by me, and others by my sons, who wore the jacket while wrestling or playing touch football in the backyard. I know it's old, but I don't want to let it go. Each time I see the Midgets jacket, I'm reminded of my youth and of my children when they were young.

The Midgets entered the basketball league run by the Bronx chapter of the YM-YWHA in our neighborhood on the Grand Concourse. The games were held in the evenings. Our team was talented. When I was sixteen, my body was fully grown. At six feet, I was taller than most of the boys my age. I didn't focus on my height, but intuitively, I felt that being taller was better than being short. Taller boys gravitate naturally to playing center in basketball, and teams expect tall boys to get rebounds.

Basketball didn't come naturally to me. My height helped, but I needed to practice every chance I could. My father bought me a basketball, and in the late afternoons, I headed to the playground to practice two essential shots: the hook shot and a turnaround jump shot. I often stayed until dark, drilling over and over until finally, I hit nothing but net. I was determined to become a better player. With my constant practice, I helped bring the Midgets to the YMHA tournament finals.

The championship game was against another neighborhood team, the Cardinals. I still remember every detail of the game. It was played in the school gymnasium at P.S. 114 on Cromwell Avenue, a few blocks from my apartment house. As we warmed up, I watched the Cardinals at the other end of the court, sizing up the competition. Their center was roughly my height. It was going to be an even game.

The Midgets won the center jump tip-off. Two passes brought the ball to me. This was my chance to start the game right. Filled with excitement, I went into the air for a turn-around jump shot—the one I had been practicing for hours on end. As I was turning toward the basket at the height of my jump, I saw that I was at the top of the free throw circle—much too far away to make the shot. With no choice then but to follow through, I let the ball go. To my never-ending amazement, the ball went through the net!

Midgets 2, Cardinals 0. What a wonderful way to start the game!

As I ran down the court on defense, I saw the gym door open, and in walked my father. *Too bad that he came late*, I thought. He had missed a wonderful opening shot. I figured he'd have plenty of chances to see me shoot during the game.

No such luck. My first shot was the only one I made for the rest of the game. I was guarded ferociously by the Cardinals center. The teams traded rebounds, passes, and points. At the end of the game, the score was tied. Everyone agreed to a sudden-death overtime period.

The Cardinals took the opening jump ball, passed three times, and threw it to their center. He was right in front of me. For the first time in the entire game, he took a hook shot.

It went in.

Game over.

The Cardinals won the championship.

What irony. I had practiced the same shot over and over for so long. Now it was used against me and my team for the other team's victory. After the game, I walked home through the park with my father. Neither of us uttered a word during the whole walk. I felt ashamed. As an adult, in the decades that followed, I often thought about that night. Why hadn't my father been able to offer any words of comfort? Even a few words of criticism would have been welcomed. Instead, total silence. At the time, I didn't know why nothing was said, and I was hurt. I carried that hurt for years.

Yes, the basketball game was important to me at the time, but I was sixteen. You may be wondering why I couldn't just get over it. I suppose that incident lingered with me because it was emblematic of the other times I looked to my father for words of wisdom or counsel, and he said nothing. I finally understand now that my father didn't talk to me that night because he didn't know what to say or do. His nurturing skills were limited, so he stayed silent. I didn't understand that then, but now, my feelings from that disappointing evening are replaced with wisdom, forgiveness, and love.

I believe that friendships require shared experience, openness, and honesty. The bonds I formed with my fellow Midgets nourished me for a long time.

As an adult, when I was a practicing certified public accountant based in Manhattan, my best friends were my partners in the large CPA firm where we worked. I socialized with them often. Our interactions daily and on weekends had many of the hallmarks of my friendships with the Midgets in my earlier years.

But then, one day, the dynamics changed. I was promoted to managing partner, a position—as the title makes clear—of management and leadership. I could feel my partner friends step away. There were two reasons: The first is that the glue that held us all together was a set of commonly held views about management, and now that included me. Money was the other major factor. I now controlled the economic lives of other partners—I decided how much they earned—and that shift in power changed how honest and open they thought they could be with me.

I truly enjoyed the role of leadership in my new position. I liked the authority that came with it. However, the change in friendships created a void not easily filled. I realized that there is some truth in the saying that it is "lonely at the top."

The Smell of Comfort

My father smoked pipes and cigars. The smell of tobacco always reminds me of my childhood. Wintertime was income tax preparation season for my father, a CPA. In that busy time, he worked a normal, six-day week, as well as two evenings a week. On two other evenings, he taught accounting at the Baruch School of The City University of New York.

Often, my father would return home late, usually well past dinner. When he was home, he smoked. When I detected the unmistakable aroma of his pipe or cigar wafting to my room, I knew Dad was in the house. Even today, whenever I smell cigar or pipe smoke, I am brought back to Walton Avenue in wintertime, a sensation that is cozy and warm.

I lost much of my sense of smell a few years ago following a concussion I sustained when I fell off a ladder. Even with my diminished ability to smell, cigar and pipe smoke comes through clearly, and with it, the feelings of wholeness and cozy family togetherness.

My mother and father were successful at raising two children, but I don't think they ever sat down and mapped out how they would do it. They led by example. I don't believe they ever discussed how their son eventually might, or ought to, earn a living. They must have hoped I'd learn such things somehow through osmosis. They never pressured me to follow in my father's footsteps and also become a CPA. Perhaps they trusted that I would make the best decision for myself. On reflection, I think I did.

My Ear to the Radio

Radio was a big deal for me growing up, as it was for many children back then. There was no television, of course. The most significant radio program, the one I enjoyed the most, was *The Lone Ranger*. Every Monday, Wednesday, and Friday at 7:30 p.m., I was glued to the radio set for a half hour, and I relished that time. The programs were riveting. They transported me to another world, the Old West, filled with good and evil morality plays.

The family had a steady evening routine: My mother would start preparing dinner around six while listening to a radio program with Henry Morgan telling funny stories. On nights when my father didn't work late, we'd be eating at quarter to seven, just as radio announcer Stan Lomax reported the day's sports scores.

I listened to everything. On weekends, it was Martin Block's *Make Believe Ballroom*, where he'd play records of the Top Forty songs of the week. As a young boy, I stood on a kitchen chair with my ear pressed against a radio on a shelf and listened to Zeke Manners and his band on New York station WNEW. That was my introduction to "country and western" music.

As I grew older, I would go to sleep with country music playing softly on my bedside transistor radio. At night, radio frequencies—especially on the AM dial—had less interference. I could pick up station WWVA in Wheeling, West Virginia almost every evening.

PAUL D. NEUWIRTH

In later years, I'd fall asleep listening to Gene Shepard, a monologist from Chicago. He told fabulous stories that went on and on about his own childhood. What great skill he had entertaining an unseen audience, all by himself, for more than an hour. From the time I was ten until I turned sixteen years old, I tuned in to radio programs on most days and evenings during the school year.

A Pinball Escapade

When I was probably eight years old, my sister and I traveled with our mother from New York City to Lock Haven, Pennsylvania, to visit our Aunt Ruth Klewans (Dad's sister) and her family. I don't recall if Pop went with us or if he arrived later.

We rode the Pennsylvania Railroad. The train was pulled by a coal-fired, steam locomotive—the iconic iron horse. When I put my head outside of the train window to see the engine, I got a cinder in my eye, but it flushed out quickly. If I close my eyes now and quietly think back to that time, I can almost hear the lullaby of the locomotive whistle and the clickety-click of the train wheels.

We stayed in Lock Haven for about a week. Aunt Ruth and Uncle Morris's house wasn't big enough to accommodate everyone, so our family slept at the Fallon Hotel, which was within walking distance of the Klewans' home.

I believe the Fallon Hotel no longer exists, but I have a vivid memory of the placement of its front desk and lobby, and especially of the best feature of the lobby: the pinball machine. At that time, pinball machines were outlawed in New York City, so this was the first time I had seen one. Mom or Dad gave me a few nickels to play the pinball games. Although I wasn't a winner the first few times I played, I understood that the slope of the machine was the main obstacle to a high score.

PAUL D. NEUWIRTH

With my last—or almost last—nickel in my pocket, I strolled to the lobby area. It was decorated with big, upholstered chairs, small tables and—as if they had been put there just for me—heavy glass ashtrays. I wandered back to the pinball machine with two of the ashtrays, turned them upside-down, and slid one under each of the machine's two front legs.

The working part of the game—where the steels balls careened off rubber posts and crashed into targets that lit up, clanged, and scored points—was not perfectly level with the ashtrays in place, but the slope was considerably less graduated. I sent the steel balls down the game board, where they meandered lazily, scoring point after point.

Playing the game with the ashtrays in place under the machine's legs was thrilling. As the points piled up, something even more exciting happened: I started to win free games. When the rigged game ended, I took away the ashtrays and played free game after free game until I was down to the last one. Then, back went the ashtrays. With limited effort, I won more free games. How long I stood at the machine is lost in my memory.

Some seven decades later, I still get the same kind of thrill at the blackjack tables in Las Vegas. There is a difference, of course: no glass ashtrays to fix the games.

There is a Right Way and There Was a Wrong Way

When it happened, I was very young—maybe five or six. It is likely that, at the time, I had a series of sore throats caused by tonsillitis. Mom, based on advice from the pediatrician who knew me, decided that my tonsils should be removed.

On the scheduled day, Mom and Dad took me to a mid-Manhattan hospital—probably French Hospital, where I was born—to have the procedure done. I would stay there overnight. I do not remember anything about the rest of that day, the hospital, the doctors, or the surgery.

What I have never forgotten, however, is the next morning. I was in a crib that was wheeled to face the hospital elevators. I was crying loudly, maybe because my throat hurt. Perhaps it was because I was in an out-of-my-control situation.

A nurse walked by. Without pausing, she said, "If you don't stop crying, your mother won't be able to see you." The nurse moved on. I stopped crying, but the effect on me of that one sentence must have been devastating.

Shortly afterward, the elevator doors opened, and there were Mom and Dad. After hugs and kisses, we went home.

During the next day, or maybe the day after, Mom hailed the Good Humor truck and asked me what kind of ice cream I'd like to have. Both she and I knew of the throat-soothing effect the cold treat would have on me. Yet I said, "No. I don't want any ice cream."

I suppose this was my indirect way of expressing my anger at Mom for putting me in *L'affaire de la Tonsil* and for letting me suffer the threat of the nurse, against which I had no defense. Being so much older and wiser now, I believe that by refusing the ice cream treat, I was also punishing myself for my passive aggression aimed at Mom.

Hot Dogs and Summer Nights

From when I was ten years old until the age of seventeen, I spent every summer at Camp Seneca in the Berkshires, a wonderful sleepaway camp. It was divided into one part for boys and one for girls. My sister went to the girls' camp.

Camp Seneca was a tidy little world, and those summers were perhaps the happiest of my youth. The days were structured, from Reveille's bugle call in the morning to Taps at night. Our team athletic competitions were interspersed with time for free play and activities to learn new skills. Boys returned annually, and campers became counselors. Fathers sent sons, sons sent grandsons. Bunks were named after Indian tribes like "Mohawk" and "Iroquois."

At Camp Seneca, I learned to shoot a rifle, to hit a target with a bow and arrow, and to use woodworking tools. I learned to play volleyball and tennis. I enjoyed being an actor in the drama group. When the days were very hot, the all-day swimming in Whaley Lake was delightful. The peaceful hours on the lake in a canoe or on a paddleboard were among the best.

When I was one of the older boys, my buddies and I eagerly looked forward to dance nights with the girls, an activity that rarely (but sometimes) led to sneaking out to meet summer girlfriends.

Mom and Dad visited twice during the eight weeks of camp, though most connection to home was maintained through mandatory daily letter writing. None of my camp friends seemed to miss their parents, and neither did I.

One summer night, probably when I was around eleven years old, the counselors piled us into the back of an open-bed truck and took us to see a movie. Along the way, the truck stopped at a general store. The counselors went inside and returned with hot dogs for us. The taste of my hot dog was unlike any flavor I knew. It was bliss on a bun. I was blown away. It was a dark night in the country, so I couldn't see what was on the hot dog, but it tasted divine.

Ten years later, I was working in Manhattan. I took the subway to the Bronx and got off at the station closest to home. I stopped at Nedick's fast food store and bought a hot dog. I looked for the mustard, but couldn't find it, so I used ketchup instead. I took a bite and WHAMO! I was back at Camp Seneca. I'd finally recreated the flavor of the hot dog I'd eaten a decade earlier on the flat-bed of the truck. *That's the taste*, I thought to myself as I devoured that hot dog at the store counter.

Over the ten years between Camp Seneca and that day in the Bronx, I had eaten plenty of hot dogs—but never with ketchup. I am still amazed that our brains can instantly recognize the memory of a taste.

Bagels and Sunday Newspapers

Right around the time of our country's bicentennial, I was in Philadelphia as the managing partner of the Philadelphia office of a CPA firm called Grant Thornton. I had started at the firm in New York as a partner in 1969. I moved to Philadelphia in 1976 to manage that office, a position I would hold for fifteen years. It would be the most satisfying professional work of my life.

Elmer R., the man I succeeded as the chief in Philadelphia, talked with me about the upcoming election for Philadelphia's city controller. He explained that the incumbent was a competent, honest man—and, in his favor, also a CPA. Elmer thought that our CPA firm should support the controller's reelection bid by donating to his campaign fund. I agreed, signed a check, and handed it to Elmer to personally deliver to the controller at City Hall later that day.

When he returned to the office, Elmer was happy. He said that the controller was pleased to receive the firm's support, and that the controller also had good news for Elmer: Our firm had won two contracts for accounting work. Elmer had picked up the signed contracts, and we could start the new work right away. This was my first week in Philadelphia, and I thought this was a good omen. I was flushed with excitement and energy, and the rest of the week went by in a flash of activity.

On Sunday, I left our new home in the Philadelphia suburb of Wynnewood to find the local bagel store. I left early because I still didn't know where to buy a bottle of milk or the Sunday newspapers. I eventually returned with everything on my list, including *The New York Times, The Philadelphia Inquirer, The Philadelphia Bulletin*, and bagels and lox.

At our family brunch, I scanned the newspaper front pages. On the first page of the *Bulletin*—in the above-the-fold lead column—was an exposé of corruption at City Hall. The story reported that a check, signed by recently arrived managing partner Paul Neuwirth of the CPA firm Grant Thornton, had been given to the city controller in exchange for two city work contracts! The story went on promising more investigative reporting to come.

At the time, it didn't occur to me that, from a public relations standpoint, this could be considered wonderful publicity. Everyone in town would quickly know who I was. Instead, I spent the rest of that Sunday in periodic states of panic. I knew that, come Monday morning, I would have to call the firm's attorney to sort everything out. I wasn't looking forward to it.

The next day, I called our attorney to ask for guidance on how to handle what I believed to be an awful situation. He was in Chicago and suggested I speak with a local attorney back in Philadelphia. "I have an old Navy buddy there, a fellow named David Sykes," the attorney said. Sykes was at the law firm Duane Morris. Never mind that he was a bankruptcy specialist.

I called David Sykes, and that was the beginning of a decades-long friendship. Dave heard my tale and sent his colleague, Marjorie (Midge) Rendell, to walk me through everything we needed to do. We found the reporter, explained that the contracts in question were bid by several

HIGHLIGHTS OF MY LIFE

companies and had been awarded to us on our merits—including that our firm was the low bidder.

What had happened was that, when Elmer brought the check to the controller, a reporter happened to be there, covering stories at City Hall. He witnessed the exchange and turned it into a corruption story. The timing of our political contribution and our contracts being awarded had been a coincidence. Nothing more linking me or my firm with political corruption ever appeared in a newspaper.

Our firm was cleared of any allegations of wrongdoing, and Midge Rendell became the attorney for any issues concerning our office. If Midge's last name sounds familiar, that's because she was married to Ed Rendell, Philadelphia's elected district attorney who later became a mayor and then a governor. Whenever I was threatened with a lawsuit, my first response was, "Please call my lawyer, Midge Rendell, the DA's wife." The issue almost always disappeared after that. Midge and I worked together on legal matters for years until she was appointed a federal judge in the U.S. bankruptcy court.

We stayed friends with the Rendells into the millennium, and they came to my wedding. In 1999, I had been living with Delaney for seventeen years. We decided that it was now or never if we were to marry. We understood that living together but not being married might easily present unwarranted legal and financial issues if either of us became ill or died. We also knew the good side of our unmarried togetherness—we knew we were staying together out of choice, without legal binding.

We learned that Philadelphia had planned a major wedding production for December 31, 1999, to be held at the convention center. All those who chose to could be married there *en masse*. We decided to take the plunge. Five hundred couples were married at that ceremony, witnessed by 10,000 of their closest friends, and officiated by His Honor, Mayor Ed

Rendell and Her Honor, Judge Midge Rendell. We had a happy reunion of sorts with their honors at the wedding. That was our last significant get-together with the Rendells.

Big cities are not strangers to corruption in city politics. I was shocked some years later when I witnessed corruption firsthand. Someone else ran for Philadelphia city controller. The candidate hosted a breakfast where he invited various CPAs in the city to hear his plan for Philadelphia. He addressed the crowd and said, "To run my campaign well, I'll need money. I'm asking you to help finance my campaign. When I'm elected, I will remember who gave me how much, and city contracts will be awarded in that proportion."

I was stunned. I walked out and felt like I needed a cold shower. It was the most blatant talk of that kind that I had ever heard. I never gave him a dime, but he was elected twice.

Beginning a Certified Public Accountant (CPA) Career and Where It Led

The Baruch School of The City College of New York (now Baruch College) is where I went to college. It is primarily a business school. I majored in accounting and graduated in 1957.

My first paid work after college, back when I was just starting out, was in Manhattan, as an auditor with a public accounting firm. As a beginner—I was a junior accountant—I felt like a sponge, learning new things every day. In those days, to get a license to practice as a CPA, one had to pass a rigorous, four-part examination and have three years of practical experience in auditing. Less than 40 percent of those sitting for the exams passed, and even fewer passed on the first try.

I spent my evenings in 1961 studying for the CPA exams and sat for them that November. I knew a man who didn't grade or influence the test scores but had access to the scores. He told me that he would let me know how I had done on the test, even before the results were released. When I mentioned that to two colleagues at the accounting firm who had taken the exams when I did, I became their "best friend." But after I learned our test results and they learned their grades from me, they disappeared. They had gotten what they wanted and had used our "friendship" for early access to information.

Easy come, easy go.

I felt pure joy to learn that I had passed the exams on my first try. What a relief not to have to put in all those hours of study anymore!

I felt so full of myself after earning a CPA license that I thought I could teach accounting to college students. So I went to Baruch College and asked the head of the accounting department for the teaching requirements. I was told that an applicant needed to have been published and to have a current CPA license, in addition to a few other small conditions. Being the detail-oriented person that I am, I made sure to meet all the prerequisites. Then I applied for the teaching job. After an interview, I was told that I didn't get the position because they wanted me to be a little older. Reapply in a few years, they said.

At that time, I wasn't just disappointed, I was angry! I called the interviewers and told them that I had seen all the other applicants who had come for an interview that day. I said that my instinct was good and it told me that I would make a better teacher than any of those other guys. I closed by saying that I expected to be hired for the college's next semester.

I was hired very shortly thereafter. Some may call that *chutzpah*, but I wanted to push hard for the job for two reasons. One was to see if I could get it. Two, I think, was to show my father, who had taught for many years, that I could do what he did.

Soon enough, there would be a third, more important reason. It turned out that I loved teaching.

Manny Saxe and Teaching

I worked as a CPA during the daytime and taught at Baruch College two nights a week, from 1962 to 1976. In the early years, I earned $8.50 an hour. Now, with four decades of hindsight, that seems such a small amount; yet it was sweet money. It was money that I used to go to the movies with my wife on Saturday nights. My teaching pay supplemented the relatively low accounting salaries of that time.

Over the years, teaching grew on me. I got to know the other instructors, especially the head of the accounting department and eventual dean of the school, Emanuel "Manny" Saxe. Manny was the same age as my father; in fact, they had been boyhood friends. Coincidentally, Manny and his wife moved into the same apartment building where I lived in Riverdale, New York, and we became good friends.

Manny wrote an accounting textbook in the 1950s. In the back of many accounting textbooks are problems about the subject matter, organized by chapter. Often, the problems are assigned to students as course homework. When Manny was working on his chapter problems for the second edition, he asked me to solve them, which I did. I was so pleased that he had the confidence to ask me.

One day, I thanked him for all the help he had given me over the years. Manny responded with two comments: First, he said that his "inventory" was people; he worked with people and their relationships with others. Then he said that nobody succeeds without standing on the shoulders of somebody else. "So don't thank me," Manny said. "Everybody does what you think I do for you." That philosophy has stayed with me all these years, because I think it's true that nobody is totally, completely self-made.

Four years passed, and I had settled into my role as an evening accounting instructor. I also changed my day job, moving to another CPA firm, the one where my father was a partner. One day, Manny called saying that Henry Sellin, a professor at NYU, was writing a book about accounting for lawyers, and Manny wanted professor Sellin to get my father to write a chapter in the new book. But, Manny said, "If you can't get the father, get the son."

Dad turned Sellin down, so the professor approached me. I accepted the assignment, and I spent the summer of 1965 writing about partnership accounting for Sellin's book *Attorney's Practical Guide to Accounting*. The book went into several editions, and I felt very proud. I'm still proud of it now. I was happy that people found value in what I wrote. Writing that chapter also affirmed that I could write well.

I highly regarded teaching in New York. I loved the idea of teaching those students in my classes at Baruch—young men and women trying to get the education that would lead to better lives. These were youngsters who fit the profile of those who traditionally attended CUNY: kids who came from limited backgrounds and whose families could not afford to send them to more costly universities. Enrolling in my class was a way for these folks to become better versions of themselves.

Since I taught in the evenings, my classes were filled with students who had finished their day jobs and then headed to me for a few hours of accounting theory. Some years, the majority of my students were from *yeshivas*, attending religious school during the day and secular school in the evening.

I am certain that I learned as much from the students in those classes as I ever taught them.

On Faith and Principles

I remember trying to make the point that if these devout Jewish students were really interested in going into the public accounting profession, it was quite possible they would not end up working for a Jewish-owned company—that is, they might be offered a job with a company that would not recognize their dietary and religious restrictions. If they were going to work at PricewaterhouseCoopers, for example, or other major CPA firms, they would be expected to finish an assignment, even if it meant hauling into work on a Saturday.

My point was that there would be times when the students' religious beliefs might come into conflict with their professional careers. I wanted to get them thinking about how they would handle those situations. I wanted these kids to understand that, in those days, the very large accounting firms just did not care about their employees' personal lives. If you couldn't work late on a Friday afternoon, the firm would find someone else who could.

I thought that the students needed to consider whether they would have to choose to work for a Jewish-owned company or to assimilate into their professional world. As I tried to raise their consciousness, it turned out that, through extensive class discussions, they raised mine.

Over the ensuing years, most workplaces developed an acceptance and tolerance of religious practices. There is now a greater recognition of the importance of work/life balance. We even have anti-discrimination laws today that require employers to accommodate people's right to worship. I see now that, in the early decades of my teaching, many of my Jewish students were ahead of the curve concerning tolerance in the professions.

My father told me a relevant story about the time, in the 1920s, that he applied for a job as a young accountant. He interviewed for a CPA position at a firm called Haskins and Sells, which later merged with other firms. The interview was going well, Dad said, but when the interviewer found out my father was Jewish, the process was effectively over.

Suddenly, somebody came into the room and handed the interviewer my father's results from an in-house exam—and he'd nailed it! The interviewer then backtracked, saying, "On reconsideration ..."

But my father already had put on his hat and was walking out the door. He took his intellect and expertise elsewhere. My father wouldn't settle for working with anti-Semites.

Just One Semester

I stopped teaching when I left New York in 1976 to work as Managing Partner in Philadelphia. I was so busy building a CPA practice in this new city that I didn't have time to teach. After a year or so, with my CPA firm work settling down a bit, I realized that I missed both teaching and interacting with students. So I called the head of the accounting department at the Wharton School of Business at the University of Pennsylvania and invited him to lunch. He came with his Number One full professor, and we had a wonderful time telling stories about college teaching.

I told them I was interested in teaching, and I said that if I wasn't the best teacher of auditing in the country, then I was pretty close to it. I said the reason for my high view of my academic talent was because I knew that I could communicate well and teach students about what I did every day to earn a living.

At almost every university, the subject of auditing is an advanced course taught by a full professor. One doesn't get to be a full, tenured professor while maintaining a successful career in public accounting. I explained, "I've done it for years, and I know that I can teach well. Also, I know the subject in all its aspects because I practice it professionally every day."

After lunch, we parted ways. They hadn't made me any offer of a teaching position at the Wharton School. I had a flashback to my first interview at Baruch, years earlier.

HIGHLIGHTS OF MY LIFE

I didn't hear from Wharton until the following September. The same professor called me on a Friday and asked, "Are you still interested in teaching?" When I said yes, he said, "Well, I've lost my professor who teaches auditing; he's going to Atlantic City to sell real estate. If you want the job, you can have it, but it's only for one semester. Classes start Monday." I was elated.

That Monday, I was in class, back doing what I loved. Every time I saw that department head in the hallway, however, he'd say, "Just one semester!"

At Penn, as at many schools, students have the opportunity to rate their instructors at the end of each course. So, at the end of the semester, I handed out the rating sheets and the students dutifully filled them out. The ratings were collected and given to Wharton's administration.

Later that week, the same professor called me and said he'd just reviewed the rating sheets, and that I was as good as I had told him.

I said, "Thank you."

He said, "Well, if you want to teach one more semester . . ."

I said, "Sure, just one more semester."

That was in 1978.

I stopped teaching in 2013. "Just one more semester" turned into more than thirty years of a most rewarding parallel career—one semester at a time.

Mountain Climbing

I have faced life's ups and downs, both personally and professionally. Everyone has. But in my work as a CPA, there were a few situations that I found to be singular.

During the summer just before my college graduation, I worked for a local accounting firm in New York. It was there that I learned an approach that is applicable to almost every assignment in the field of public accounting. I came to understand that, before beginning any work, one needs to know specifically the nature of the task, how it is expected to be done, how long it should take to complete, and if it might it be done better if done differently. These guidelines are valid in most lines of work. Learned early, these steps became part of a solid business foundation for me.

After college graduation, I got a position at a larger CPA firm, Eisner & Lubin, based in Manhattan. I spent four years with this fine firm. I started as a "junior accountant," a term now generally replaced by "assistant accountant." As part of my employment, I was required to sign an agreement stating that, if I ever left this CPA firm, I would not take any of their clients with me. It was known that my father was a partner at another CPA firm, and Eisner & Lubin (E&L) wasn't about to take any chances with me siphoning off their business.

E&L, still in business today, was a terrific place for me to start my public accounting career. I learned so much of the technical and professional elements of being a public accountant. It was good training and enjoyable work, and I found that I was good at it.

Four years later, I left to work for another firm, called Klein, Hinds & Finke (KH&F)—the place where my father was a partner. The cultural differences in the two firms came as a rude awakening. In the four years I'd spent at Eisner & Lubin, I'd only had a total of four days of unassigned time. By contrast, KH&F didn't keep its employees quite so busy; extra staff was carried so nobody had to hustle. We were allowed to take our time completing assignments.

At Eisner & Lubin, if I managed a two-week assignment that required a four-person staff, I invariably received a phone call from management on the Thursday of the first week saying that I had to release half my staff. I would push back, but ultimately agree to let one person go to another client. In any event, I would be short-staffed and my assistants would each have more work to do in a shorter period of time.

When I got to KH&F, things were very different. I liked the pleasant, relaxed family atmosphere at my new company. If I was assigned four people for *two* weeks on an engagement and they spent *three* weeks with all four staff, it didn't seem to matter. It almost seemed as if nobody was watching the CPA firm's bottom line.

And yet, despite the differences in staffing style, Klein, Hinds & Finke managed to remain a profitable company. My father told me that, during the Great Depression of the 1930s, his firm had major difficulty in collecting client fees. However, even then, the firm did not reduce staff. The partners told employees, "We can't pay you now, but we'll give you subway fare so you can come and go, and when things get better, we'll make it up to you." And that's what they did.

That kind of loyalty was unusual back in the 1960s when I was there, and is practically unheard of today. After KH&F was sold in 1969 to

Grant Thornton, the staff who had worked at Klein Hinds & Finke held reunions every two years or so for at least a decade, because they had such an affinity for each other that had been fostered by the company. I admit that I found the comradeship rather unexpected and truly touching.

If Klein, Hinds & Finke was profitable, why was it sold? Well, the nine owners, including my father and me, were getting older. I think that the three most senior partners didn't sufficiently trust the other six to run the firm well after they retired. These older partners were thinking specifically about the security of their own retirement income.

So, on August 1, 1969, the KH&F partners who controlled the firm sold it to Grant Thornton (GT), a CPA firm with offices all around the United States. Two months later, in October, Grant Thornton held its annual partners meeting. This was the first of many GT meetings I would attend in the following years. This one was held in the Marco Polo Hotel in Hallandale, Florida. Partners flew in from all over the country.

Picture the scene: In southern Florida's off season, a group of unattached, well-to-do men gathered in an otherwise empty hotel. Their presence was like catnip to kittens: the place became flooded with working women looking for love and money. I was more interested in the business of the day.

The Grant Thornton CEO went through the normal procedural course of events, and then he announced that the firm's profit for the year (which had ended on the past July 31) was $13 per share. That struck me as odd, because the partners at my firm (KH&F) had been promised $16 per share as part of the sale negotiations.

A few minutes later, during a coffee break, I approached the former KH&F partners and asked, "Did you hear what they just said? We were promised $16 per share, and they only earned $13. I think we ought to pack our bags and go home!"

I thought the merger should be voided. Either we were being lied to, or the folks at Grant Thornton were not able to produce what they promised. Whatever the reason, I urged that we should leave and go back to practicing public accounting on our own. But most of the senior partners, including my father, were frightened about the potential loss of retirement income. They couldn't bring themselves to void or renegotiate the terms of the sale of their firm.

My father and his fellow partners knew they might have been duped, but they felt that had no place to go. They understood that, if they left GT now, they would be back in the position of retiring from an accounting firm where they didn't have faith in those remaining to run the firm to provide them with a secure retirement. After some heated back and forth, we all agreed to stay.

At the end of the week-long conference, I returned to New York. I visited my new GT partners and said, "You promised $16 per share. I want it. I want my income to be based on $16 per share, and not $13." They were taken aback, but I was ready to leave if they wouldn't agree to my request.

It didn't occur to me, then or ever, that I would unable to earn a living. If my career wasn't going to be with GT, I was confident that I'd find work elsewhere. Truth be told, I didn't care whether GT agreed to my request or not. Even though the extra money would be nice, the three-dollar difference wasn't going to make me overly wealthy or send me to the poorhouse.

Money wasn't my main reason for insisting Grant Thornton honor its commitment. I'm not a pushover, and I wanted my new partners to know that. I wanted them to honor their promises. And they did! The other eight partners who came to Grant Thornton with me were paid $13 a share—but I got $16.

My need to stand tall continued. When GT reallocated partner holdings—which means partners' individual percentage of profits were changed, based on performance—I was told that my holdings would go up. But the change was minuscule. I said, "Keep it. That's not enough. You're not giving me enough to make any difference in my earnings. Either give me what I should get, or don't give me anything, because I won't accept what you're offering."

Again, I knew I would always find work, and I wanted the company to do the right thing and not screw me over. After that little chat, Grant Thornton paid me more. That's how things began, and that's how they went.

The combination of the Klein, Hinds & Finke and Grant Thornton accounting firms brought with it an unintended consequence. KH&F was the independent auditor of the American Institute of Certified Professional Accountants (AICPA). Founded in 1887, the institute is the national professional organization of certified public accountants in the United States, with more than 418,000 members.

For the two years through June 30, 1969, I had been the KH&F partner in charge of a very prestigious engagement: the audit of the AICPA's financial statements. But when KH&F and GT merged, a GT partner became the president of the AICPA. The combined accounting firms were then deemed not to be independent of the client, so we had to give up doing its auditing.

As a sop to KH&F and to me, I was made a member—one of four—of the AICPA Insurance Committee, and I soon became its chairman, a position I held from 1970 to 1982. This committee monitors the life, disability, and long-term care insurance programs for AICPA members and their families, making sure that the coverage, features, and services of the programs exceed expectations. I am proud that on my watch, CPA life insurance grew to be the largest group life program in the United States offering affordable protection for members.

I was reasonably good at being an auditor. I think you may be familiar with what a public accounting auditor does. He or she examines the records of a client to see if the numbers the client shows in its financial statements are in accordance with Generally Accepted Accounting Principles. Over a period of years, I eagerly learned the how-to-do-it skills of auditing.

Among my assigned audits were the financial statements of a New Jersey distillery and liquor and wine importer. I was the Number Two person on that audit team, and the lead fellow was doing most of the work. "Let me relieve you of some of that," I said. I knew that if I were to take on his tasks, he'd have to show me the techniques of how to do what he was doing. In that way, I would learn new skills. He looked at me and replied, "If I teach you, there won't be anything for me to do."

I thought he was taking a stupid approach to the work—but I knew that eventually, I would figure out on my own how to do what he was doing. And I did. Looking back now, I realize that I didn't like to do repetitive work. I wanted new and different challenges all the time.

Several years later, one of the largest clients of our New York office was scheduled to have its financial statements audited, and the man who had led the audit team for years suddenly took another job. GT was left scrambling—who would make the most sense to put in charge of this large client engagement?

The firm took a reasonable course of action: Two people were selected to lead the audit team—a partner nearing retirement and me. GT's managing partners went to the client and said, "We'll give you an older man with a great deal of experience and also somebody younger who's filled with piss and vinegar. That way, you'll have the best of both worlds."

But the client was smarter. Its chairman said, "I don't care which one you give us, but we only want one auditor, so we know who to hold responsible." The accounting firm picked me. It was to be a baptism by fire.

I learned that the client company was headquartered in Florida, with subsidiaries spread out all over the world. It was a massive global conglomerate making food blenders, radar gun directors for battleships, air conditioning vents, and all sorts of massive machinery. When I was told that I was to be in charge of the audit, I remember thinking, *Holy smokes! I've never audited anything this big before!*

To tell the truth, I wasn't so sure I could do it, so I corralled a younger man in the office who I knew to be a good auditor. I said, "Charlie, I want you to help me with this. You and I will plan the work, you will direct most of the day-to-day audit fieldwork, and if you need any help, we will resolve the issues together. Just call me." Charlie obligingly went down to Florida, and sure enough, right around Christmas, I received a call from him.

"You'd better get down here, Paul," Charlie said. "I think I found financial fraud."

Trying to book a flight out of LaGuardia at Christmastime was like trying to walk on water. Finally, Pan Am rolled out an unscheduled flight because so many customers wanted to fly. The flight arrived in Miami, and I needed to get to Boca Raton. *I'll rent a car*, I thought. No such luck; all the rental cars were already in use.

I finally managed to hail a taxi. I remember asking the driver if he could turn off the meter and let me pay him a flat fee, but he said, "No way!" He sure had a merry Christmas with that fare.

In any event, I rolled up to a fancy hotel in Boca Raton at about two in the morning. I made it to my room, where the previous guest had forgotten half a tub of ice cream in the freezer. That was my dinner. Then I crashed on the bed, still fully clothed.

I met my colleague, Charlie, the next morning. As I reviewed his work, it was clear that there was indeed evidence of fraud. The company was incorrectly overstating its profit. I checked the work sufficiently to know that the financial statements had to be changed. Instead of showing a profit for the year, the company would show a loss.

I also knew that showing a loss rather than a profit would lead to a disastrous domino effect: Banks would call in their loans, and the company would likely have to file for bankruptcy.

When I told my partners in New York of the situation, they had the view that, if the client indeed went bankrupt, our accounting firm might be sued by the client for some made-up issue of professional malpractice. I believed that, even though there would be a downside for the client and also potentially for my accounting firm, the financial accounts should show the truth.

Word spread quickly to GT's headquarters in Chicago. I received a telephone call from Grant Thornton's second-in-command executive, who told me that he wanted me to speak with his top technical accountant. That individual said he thought that I had audited incorrectly, and that the client company's financial statements *should* be showing a profit.

After long telephone exchanges, I finally said, "You sign our firm's report letter, because I won't."

The next day, the number two man and his top technical accountant arrived in New York and started their own, in-depth review of the audit work. They told me why my view of the accounting was incorrect. Moreover, they said that they were both more experienced than I and also much smarter. They suggested I follow their advice.

I understood the real reason these fellows flew in from Chicago to get me to change my mind: My calculations suggested that the company would go bankrupt, and this was our firm's largest client. Imagine the mess that would follow! Loss of fees and a high likelihood of being sued were all part of the equation.

But even after hearing all that, I still couldn't agree to attest to the financial statements unless they were adjusted to show the loss. I refused to sign off on the Auditors' Opinion.

As I walked down the office hall, distraught and discouraged, Howard G.—the chief technician in GT's New York office—stopped and asked what was going on. I told him all about the auditing fiasco, and he said, "I'll handle it. You go sit down somewhere."

Howard managed to convince the other accountants that my approach was the right way. The audited financial statements ended up showing a loss for the Florida conglomerate. The client's bank loans were called, leading quickly to a bankruptcy filing. And, yes, there was a huge mess in court for a while, although GT came out winning the case against it. I had to be satisfied with knowing that I had directed the audit of a huge company's financial statements, and I'd gotten it done with the right—though unpleasant—results.

After this episode, I knew that I could use the experience I'd gained in auditing a worldwide conglomerate to lead an audit of just about any company—even one as large as General Motors. Figuratively, I had climbed the highest mountain in my professional world. I also knew immediately that I didn't *want* do this kind of work anymore. I knew that everything else in auditing would be just a variation on a theme I had already played.

Having climbed a professional Mount Everest, would scaling a series of smaller peaks still be satisfying? Or would I keep hiking up the same tall mountain? Could I do either? Yes. Did I want to? No! I no longer felt the satisfaction I had enjoyed in my work. The thrill was gone.

This particular event happened in 1972 when I was thirty-six years old. I knew I needed a change of scenery.

My Journey in Marketing

Historically, CPAs—like other professionals—have built a wall around themselves and called it a code of ethics. For many decades, this ethical code, among other restraints, prohibited CPAs from advertising and from soliciting the clients of another CPA firm.

Most of the major accounting firms paid lip service to these requirements, although they competed for new clients—sometimes openly and more often subtly. Companies charged by professional societies with flouting the ethics rules usually said they would not do it again, but then they went on as before.

The bans on marketing by CPAs were lifted when the federal government said that, if the code of ethics wasn't changed to allow marketing, the CPA profession might be held liable for restraint of trade and subject to penalties. The accounting profession adapted quickly to allow marketing.

Many people went into public accounting specifically because of the prohibitions on marketing. This self-selecting group wanted to practice a technical skill but didn't want to "dirty their hands" in the marketplace. The position of the federal government and the following change in CPA ethical rules opened up new permissiveness that some accountants didn't like, even though it also presented more opportunity in the public accounting world.

It became clear that the elimination of the rules against openly selling CPA services presented both an opportunity and a real need for CPAs to do this marketing of professional services. Just as I was thinking that I didn't want to continue as an auditor for the rest of my career, I was asked to take charge of marketing for GT's New York office. The timing could not have been sweeter. It took me all of about two seconds to say yes.

My work shifted from being an auditor of client financial statements to being a marketer of professional services. Overnight, I was in charge of creating marketing plans and leading the people around me to buy into the new programs.

My partners in New York thought I was mad. They thought that the only security for a public accountant lay in relationships with clients. If you're doing marketing, they said, time constraints will force you to give up those client relationships. Why would you let go of the opportunity to work with CEOs and decision-makers? Where's the financial security in marketing?

But I didn't care what they said. I was optimistic that if it didn't work out, I'd find another way to earn a living.

The new field was exciting for me on two counts: First, it got me out of auditing, the work that I had done for the last 15 years, and second, I didn't know a thing about marketing. That meant I'd have to learn—which was an exciting prospect. This was a new mountain I was very willing to climb.

I was a marketer in New York from 1972 to 1976. I was in charge of creating a marketing program for the New York office of my firm, and I was also responsible for getting the program implemented. This was a new issue for the whole public accounting profession as well as for the professionals in my firm.

We all learned to take a closer look at where our new business came from. For the first time for most of us, we documented how much of our time was spent in activities that were likely to produce new business.

We soon realized that most of our new business came through referrals from bankers and lawyers, so those professions became our relationship targets. To build those relationships, I spent much of my time over lunches and dinners and at sporting events with these potential referrers, describing what my firm was all about. I explained to them how GT could help their clients.

Marketing included public relations activities to get GT's name recognized and well-thought-of by those who could refer business. Our office also produced seminars and educational programs for bankers and lawyers. We learned about the concept of reciprocity—if you refer business to me, I'll refer business to you. We kept score of who sent us clients and to whom we sent business.

Like most of the public accounting profession at that time, we were amateurs at marketing, but we kept plugging away at it because it was a necessity. We learned how to do it. Some of our efforts did not produce good results and were scrapped, while other methods were unexpectedly successful. In the five years that I was the partner in charge of marketing our services, the New York office grew in client size and in profitability. In the end, that is probably the truest test of success for any marketing program.

This was also during the period when GT was expanding into Europe and developing its international firm. International accounting firms are structurally different from other industrial, multinational companies. Firms like Pricewaterhouse and Grant Thornton and other very large, U.S.-based public accounting firms found ways to work with non-U.S. accounting companies under an international "brand" like Grant Thornton International (GTI).

Although there might be a GTI member firm in Italy, Ireland, India, Switzerland, and the United States, the firms are not integrated with one another and are not stockholders in each other. The advantage of being part of one company brand is that, if there is public accounting work to be done for, say, an American client company with a subsidiary in Switzerland and in Italy, the Swiss and Italian GTI member firms can do the non-U.S. work in Europe and opine on that work while the U.S. member firm can take responsibility for the work done on the parent company's accounts.

At one point, GT approached me and asked if I would become the firm's man in Paris to oversee international work in Europe and to resolve disputes among GTI member firms, should they arise. I said no. My excuse was that I thought it would not be wise for my three children to grow up in France and then return to the States as quasi-Frenchmen.

In hindsight, I think that might not have been the best decision. We all probably would have developed a greater appreciation for the larger world. Who knows where that might have led my children? My wife at the time spoke fluent French, and she would have fit right in.

But the real reason I declined the offer was that I was scared. I thought that without staff and without a direct line of authority to the U.S., I would be out on a limb all by myself. In corporate America, that's never a good place to be.

C'est la vie.

Soon enough, the company asked me if I'd like to be in charge of our Philadelphia branch office, which was losing money. It seemed like a good opportunity. It meant that I could be an entrepreneur, building a business without having to invest large amounts of capital.

I made the transition from five years of being a marketer to becoming a managing partner. In an accounting firm, managing partners are kings in their offices. Whatever the managing partner says generally goes. There is almost no appeal of a managing partner's decisions, as long as that office is highly profitable.

I thought I'd be happy in Philadelphia. I came to the new city with the charge of taking a small and little-known CPA firm and building it into a large and profitable professional office. This became my work for the next 15 years.

A Tale of Two Cities

I found Philadelphia in 1976 to be so different from New York. People in the city and suburbs of Philadelphia didn't have the same relationship with their city that New Yorkers have with New York.

In New York, my office was in a high-rise on Sixth Avenue and 47th Street. I had a clear view of the Hudson River. Seeing the ships coming and going symbolized the New Yorker's expansive worldview to me. Everybody was interested in what everybody else was doing: "Where'd you get this shirt? What's that new restaurant around the corner, have you tried it? What's new, what's hot?" No matter where you lived, Manhattan was home, and where you lay your head at night was simply a bedroom.

Philadelphia then was vastly different. I moved to a quiet, western suburb called Wynnewood. Some of my partners lived there, too, and I remember asking them, "Do you want to go into town tomorrow night?"

They'd look at me and ask, "Why?"

I'd shrug and say, "To go to a nice restaurant."

"Why would you want to do that?" was their response.

I didn't understand it, but Philadelphians were just less involved with their big city. People went into the city to work, and then they came home. Center City back then felt like a grainy, gritty, second-rate downtown. "Filthadelphia" was a well-earned nickname. The grit and grime has long been replaced by glittering high-rises and chic dining destinations, but that transformation was only starting to get underway when I arrived in 1976.

I can't complain about my commute to Philadelphia. The first day I headed to work from Wynnewood, my wife drove me to the commuter rail station and I boarded the train. I opened my *Wall Street Journal*, prepared to go through it cover-to-cover before arriving. I hadn't finished scanning the first page before hearing the conductor say, "Center City, last stop, everybody out."

I couldn't believe it! When I lived in Riverdale, no matter what route I took to get to 47th Street and Sixth Avenue—whether I jumped on the express bus at 239th Street, took Metro North into town, or drove—covering a distance of 12 miles took me an hour and a quarter, door-to-door. Traveling from Wynnewood to my office in Philadelphia took 15 minutes, tops. When I drove, I'd tune in to the local Philadelphia traffic reporter, and often he would say, "Avoid the highway, it's barely crawling." I'd be cruising along thinking he didn't know what "slow" was! I suppose traffic speed is relative.

Two very quick anecdotes may show how pigeon-holed these Philadelphia suburbs were. My wife was an avid tennis player. One day, she saw our neighbor across the street carrying a tennis racket into her home. She went across the street, knocked on the door, introduced herself and said, "I'd like to invite you to my country club, whenever it's good for you. We can have lunch there and play tennis."

To my wife's astonishment, the woman said, "You know, if I say yes, then I'm going to have to invite you to play with me at my club. I just don't want to add any more people to my group. Thank you, but no." My wife was dumbfounded. We had never heard such a strange thing!

Our son, Richard, was age seven when we first arrived in Wynnewood. Our new home was still under construction, and he headed into the neighborhood to explore. He went down the hill and almost immediately came back up to the house. The color was gone from his face and his lips quivered.

"Richard, what's wrong?" I asked.

He said, "Dad, I went down the street and I saw a boy who looked about my age. I went over to him and said, 'My name is Richard, I'm new here. Would you like to be friends?' The boy said, 'No, I have enough friends.'"

I think those two anecdotes described some of the culture in the Philadelphia suburbs in 1976. If I said to somebody I knew, "I've been invited to a party in Jenkintown, and I can bring a guest," I would likely hear: "Well that's on the other side of the river, I don't think I want to do that." At gatherings—a Saturday night dance at the country club, for example—the conversations were about high school basketball games that the men had played or gone to during their teenage glory days.

My new city was not what I would call an outreaching kind of society. I came to see it as an extension of Quaker Philadelphia. Edward Baltzell, a professor at the University of Pennsylvania who studied White Anglo-Saxon Protestant culture, wrote a book about Puritans in Boston and Quakers in Philadelphia. Both groups were decidedly upper crust, but the main difference between them was that, though Puritans and Quakers set out to make money, Bostonians (ostensibly) felt guilty about it and put much money back into the city. They built museums or a library, obliquely saying, "Look at what I did." That was the Kennedy family's approach to life.

Philadelphia Quakers didn't feel the need to take credit for enriching their city. Self-aggrandizement is frowned upon among Quakers. It seemed to me that, in the City of Quakers, it was just fine to make money. However, if one wanted to build a mansion, their goal was to build it outside of the city, put a wall around it, and never brag about it.

I came to Philadelphia during the era when Frank Rizzo was the mayor. Police were predominant—Rizzo had been a police commissioner before becoming mayor. In hindsight, it seems like once a week I would read in the newspapers that the police had killed somebody. They'd be in pursuit of someone wanted for a crime and he would end up dead.

True, violence occurred on many street corners. It was a rare day that someone was not mugged while walking home or taking public transportation. I was accustomed to New York, where the crime rate had dropped radically. I knew that if I got stopped by a cop in Philadelphia—which I did, for going through a stop sign—I should keep my hands on top of the steering wheel and answer "Yes, sir" to whatever the police asked. Otherwise, there was a possibility *I'd* end up dead. That might be an exaggeration, but that's how I felt.

My first secretary in Philadelphia, Jackie, was a lovely woman in her late twenties. One day, our conversation got around to my asking whether she had been to New York.

"No," she replied.

"Have you ever been to Washington?" I asked.

"No," she said again.

I continued, "You live right between two major metropolitan areas and you haven't been to either city?"

She looked at me and said, "Why would I want to go? Everything I need or want is right here."

She lived in a house next to her mother's house and all her friends were there in South Philadelphia. That was her world. She had the social characteristics of someone from a small town. In those years of the mid-1970s, I found her not atypical for Philadelphians!

HIGHLIGHTS OF MY LIFE

In the decades since then, Philadelphia has seen a great expansion. New construction abounds, and the mind-set has expanded as well. Today, Philadelphians have pride in their city. The center of town is now filled with dozens of new restaurants. The city is much cleaner and safer than it was 40 years ago. Housing costs are dramatically lower than in New York, and that is no longer a secret. Young professionals and many people involved in the arts have flocked to Philadelphia for its economics and lifestyle.

In 1976, my CPA firm was located at 16th and Market Streets in a high-rise office building. The firm had nicely appointed offices, and at first, I wondered where I was going to sit. I didn't want to be a jerk and tell the managing partner I was replacing to get out of his room so I could sit in his spot. Instead, I found a small, empty room in the big office, and I made that my space. I knew that my strength and effectiveness wouldn't depend on the size of the room I used.

I found that the rent for the whole office was very high and there was no expansion space possible. From the window of my office on 16th and Market, I could see a building that looked newly finished over at 20th and Market Streets. Though it was plainly designed, the new building was a nice, modern high-rise.

"Why don't we move there?" I asked one of my partners.

"Oh, we can't," he answered.

"Why?"

"That's four blocks away."

He wasn't kidding! His answer described the comfort zone that Philadelphians looked for. Their attitude was, if one had an old hat that fit well, why would they want to get a new one?

The Chinese Wall

Around 18th Street or thereabouts there had been the Filbert Street Viaduct. It was disparagingly referred to as the "Chinese Wall" because it divided the center of the city in half and took up blocks of valuable real estate in the heart of Philadelphia. It also stunted economic growth in the northern and western corners of the city.

Traffic in that area was always a nightmare because the short stone archways that ran across the streets blocked anything taller than a midsize vehicle. Eventually, the railroad tracks the wall had carried were moved underground, and the viaduct was demolished in the 1950s—but for long-time city dwellers, that dividing line was symbolic. It went across Market Street. On the east side of the wall, business was done. West of the wall was considered wasteland.

I hadn't put these realizations together when my partner initially expressed disinterest in moving four blocks from our current offices. To long-time residents, those four blocks were like going to another world, and it took Philadelphians a long time to get over the perceived stigma.

I became convinced, however, that the space in the newer office building four blocks away was a good location for the Grant Thornton office, so I pushed the proposal forward. I signed a lease at the 20th Street building. Then I shifted our focus to designing an office that

HIGHLIGHTS OF MY LIFE

would be comfortable and attractive, where work could be completed efficiently.

I hired a fabulous designer named Kenneth Parker who had a big design business in town. He designed an office that, in my view, was spectacular. All the rooms had angled walls. There was not a square room anywhere in the plan. Parker designed the offices with a lot of glass so you could see who was inside each room. Some people didn't care for that, but I thought it was wonderful. Office designers thought so, too.

Parker's work was featured on the cover of *Office Magazine*. His design for our space worked well for us. The flow was great. I was happy every time I went in to work.

A Domino Effect

The Ladies Auxiliary of the Medical College of Pennsylvania ran a fundraising event where, for a fee, groups visited offices that they wouldn't otherwise be able to see. A nice woman came to see me because she had heard about our new office. She asked if I would mind the office being on their tour.

"Mind? Of course not!" I replied. I immediately thought about the good publicity. "What else do I have to do to participate?"

She said, "Nothing. On the evening of the tour, you go home. We'll take care of everything." And they did.

This same woman talked to her husband, the chairman of the board of the Medical College of Pennsylvania. She told him that he ought to get me on his board.

When I was asked, I said, "Yes, I can contribute professional expertise, but do you expect me to contribute large amounts of money as part of my service on the board?" They said no.

"Well, then count me in!" I responded.

That was another big difference between Philadelphia and New York. My father had been invited to be on the board of a medical school—I don't remember which university it was associated with, but it was a New York school. He declined because of the financial commitment that he thought he would have had to make.

HIGHLIGHTS OF MY LIFE

I was on the MCP board for about 20 years, and it was a wonderful experience. I believe that, as chairman of its finance committee, I made a major contribution to the success of the institution. Eventually, MCP was purchased by a group in Pittsburg that mismanaged it into bankruptcy.

Was I pleased with my new life in Philadelphia? I was building what was essentially a new public accounting practice, teaching at the Wharton School of the University of Pennsylvania, participating on the board of the Medical College of Pennsylvania, and being in a new place where adventure waited around the next corner. Yes, it was a fine time for me.

As much as I absorbed life in Philadelphia, I brought a New York mentality to my firm. One day, I met with one of my colleagues, a manager who was one rank below the level of partner. This manager had been holding onto a report for a client for a very long time, even though just about all our work was done.

When asked why, she replied, "Well, in order for us to release this report, we have to get a letter from the client's lawyer saying whether there are lawsuits against the client that the lawyer is handling, and how much money the lawyer is owed."

I said, "Well, that's normal."

"The lawyer is on vacation," my colleague continued. "And when he comes back, we'll contact him and get the letter and then issue our report to the client."

I said, "I don't think that's a good idea. What I'm used to, and what I want you to get used to, is when something has a due date or something needs to be delivered, do what it takes to deliver it—now. Don't be the one that everybody else is waiting on. That will always end badly. Let's be known for on time or early delivery."

"What about the lawyer?" she asked.

I said, "Call the lawyer's secretary and find out where he is. Have her call him there and have him call you. Tell him what you need, that you need it now, and get him to make it happen." She did that and we issued the report the next day.

Change was high on my list. I couldn't stand the slow pace. I was ready to speed things up, and I had a new rallying cry: "Not in this office, not anymore. Get it done now. Keep the client happy. Give the client a satisfying experience of how we do business. And then, when the time is right, ask the client to recommend you to somebody else."

This was a period starting in 1976, and the pace was slow—glacial, in my opinion. I think that I contributed to the change in the business culture in Philadelphia. Certainly there was change in my office.

Although it was not an original thought with me, I believed that one of my main tasks was to make sure I had the right people to work with. If somebody didn't or couldn't or wouldn't work at a pace that got things done, I asked them to leave and replaced them with somebody who could and would. My office became transformed by the talented people I was able to hire.

I had come to Philadelphia to replace someone who had managed that facility for a long time. He and I had different philosophies. He believed, "If you have a lot of small clients and you lose one, it's not so terrible. If you have big clients and you lose one, look out!"

I said, "Having a lot of small clients is no fun. Who wants to be an accountant to gas stations?"

His answer was, "Well, gas stations pay their bills."

I wanted bigger, more profitable clients, and he didn't want to go in that direction. So I asked him to retire. Over time, I changed the office culture to one that got things done *now*, to serve the needs of larger, more profitable businesses.

 I have grown to love Philadelphia. Following a marital separation and divorce, I moved from Wynnewood to the heart of the city. The Philadelphia suburbs are beautiful, but it's also quite lovely where I live now. From where Delaney and I have our townhouse, if you walk through the courtyard, out under the arch, and take a right, you're on 2nd Street. If you go to the left, you're on Front Street.

 If you were to go one more block, you'd be on what used to be called Delaware Avenue, now called Columbus Boulevard, and you're at the Delaware River. The city hosts fireworks on the river every New Year's Eve and Fourth of July. We can see them from our roof deck. We go down to the river often. Delaney walks to the shops, and the clerks know her by name. We live in Philadelphia's Queen Village. It's a fine community.

Sometimes More Than a Hired Hand

Throughout my career, I found that most of my clients considered me a "hired hand." I was a skilled professional, pleasant and adept at maintaining solid relationships, but few clients would have considered me a close friend. No matter who they were, I did my work the same way. Those clients who became my friends were precious to me.

In some measure, the nature of my professional work made client friendships either awkward or prohibitive. As an auditor of a client's financial statements and as the head of the office performing the audit, I had to maintain independence from the clients, both of mind and in fact. This requirement created a barrier against many close, shared experiences, which are the foundations of friendship.

The clients I worked for were, for the most part, talented, lovely folks. They were people I could learn from and who I enjoyed being with. There is a difference, though, between enjoying someone's presence and developing an actual friendship. Sometimes, my experiences with clients were just wonderful.

As an example of singular experiences with clients, I recall PA Consulting, a British company. It had a spectacular, futuristic-looking office in New Jersey. I oversaw their independent auditing work. In their offices one day, the officer in charge of U.S. operations said that he had a visitor arriving from a big German company. He thought it might be interesting if I eavesdropped on their conversation.

    I did. It was an amazing interaction. The man from Germany had come to get a tour of the beautiful New Jersey facility. We headed to the laboratory where the U.S. manager showed the German a newly developed porcelain sink. To me, it looked like any ordinary sink.

    "There's soap over there. Would you wash your hands?" my client asked his German visitor. The man washed and he rinsed, but there were no towels.

    "Put your hands over the sides of the sink," instructed the client. On each side of the sink were a couple of vents where forced air blew, drying hands or whatever else might be put over them.

    "How lovely!" said the German. This was just before forced hot-air hand dryers were going mainstream, so they weren't nearly as popular as they are today.

    My client reached into his pocket and said, "Here, these are for you. They are patent papers for the sink you just used. It's yours."

    The German was impressed, but he had something else in mind. "The sink is very nice, but what we really need is a toilet that uses two pints of water instead of two gallons. Can you do that?"

    "I think so."

    "Can you have it to Germany in a month?"

    "Yes."

    I was blown away by that exchange. My client was giving away something of value, but in exchange, he had received a large order from the German visitor. For me it was a live demonstration of a variation on giving away a razor to sell blades. It was an important lesson in a very good way to do business.

I've had these kinds of experiences throughout my life—seeing what people do, and how they do it. Looking back, I realize that over the decades of my career, I learned all sorts of new and useful things from almost every client.

An Uncommon Man

From time to time, at the dinner table, Dad would tell interesting stories about one of his tax clients, Mr. J. M. (Jack) Kaplan. Near December one year, Jack offered to send our whole family on a Florida vacation, free of charge. Dad was grateful for the offer, but he refused the gift, saying that the professional fees he charged were sufficient and nothing more was needed. Jack asked my Dad to send me to see him. At the time, I was a fourteen-year-old in junior high school.

Jack's office was in the Wall Street area, and it is there that I went to meet him. I wore what I considered to be stylish clothes: grey gabardine slacks, a green nylon shirt, suede loafers and, to top it all, pink socks. Jack took one look at me and called his secretary, Carl who was a high-level, personal assistant. Jack told Carl, "take him to lunch and get him some clothes."

Carl and I had lunch in a fancy restaurant nearby and then he took me to Brooks Brothers. He told the salesman, "Measure him and get him a good suit." When the Brooks Brothers standard three-piece grey flannel suit had been fitted, we went down the street to Rogers Peet, where he bought some dress shirts for me.

Then I was sent home. Eventually, my new clothes arrived. I disliked the grey flannel suit and refused to wear it. After many months, I decided to put on the suit, and I wore it periodically over several years. It was made of such strong fabric, I could not wear it out.

As it always does, time passed. Some 15 years later, when I was working as a certified public accountant in Dad's firm, I was assigned to do accounting and tax work for one of Dad's clients: the same J. M. Kaplan.

I renewed my acquaintance with him and Carl, who was still his assistant. It was at this time that I learned of Jack's enormous wealth and influence. I was stunned when, one day at his office, I heard Jack ask Carl to get the president on the telephone! In less than two minutes, the President of the United States was on the other end of the line talking with Jack.

I learned about details of Jack's portfolio. Among other investments, at one time he had owned Hearn Department Stores and bought the Welch's Grape Juice Company. His philanthropy was renowned for its largess, inventiveness, and diversity. All of this, I learned, was done by a self-made man who grew up poor. In his youth, he'd sold soap in the streets near Boston to help feed his family.

While I did some income tax work for Jack's companies, I saw how investment bankers periodically called Jack to suggest stock market assets. When asked how much Jack should invest, he might be told, "Until we ask that you stop buying." I surmised that, if the investment turned out well, both Jack and the investment banker were happy; if the investment created a loss, Jack believed that he would receive information about another company in which he would make profits that more than covered his earlier losses.

In the mid-1960s, I read a front page story in *The New York Times* about Rep. Wright Patman. The article focused on whether U. S. government money given to certain tax-exempt foundations was used to pay for overseas spies for the United States. The news story also named some small companies owned by Jack.

Intrigued, and wanting to know more, I went to Jack's office. The several corporate names that had been in gold leaf lettering on the glass door of his office the day before had been removed. When I asked to see the accounting ledgers of these companies, I was told that they were no longer available in that office.

Eventually, the congressional investigation into the movement of money to finance spies ended with no significant results. I never learned about the involvement, if any, of the companies that were named in the *New York Times* story, but I have wondered about this issue for half a century.

A Man of the World

In the summer of 1994, Delaney and I joined my cousin Eddie and his mate Judy on a marvelous, two-week trek through the Swiss Alps—a highlight of our travels. After climbing, walking, and camping in the mountains and small towns, we spent our last Swiss day in Zurich, lodging at a fine hotel. Following a relaxing boat ride on Lake Zurich, we found and explored the hotel Baur au Lac because I had heard about it years earlier from a client, Professor Gert von Gontard.

Gert had a singular life. He was the grandson of Clara Busch, who married an Anheuser. Together, they owned and operated the Anheuser Busch brewery in St. Louis.

Gert grew up in Munich, Germany, where he published two magazines: one about theater and the other an anti-Nazi publication. One day, in the early 1930s, he learned that his name was on the police "blacklist." Fearing arrest, he left Germany that day via Swissair. His destination was the Hotel Baur au Lac, from where he contacted his grandmother, who wired him enough money for travel to the United States.

With a keen interest in theater, Gert amassed a library of Playbills of all Broadway offerings from the 1920s to the 1940s. After World War II, he produced the first German-language theater in Jerusalem, and he brought German-language theater to the United States and purely American theater to Germany.

HIGHLIGHTS OF MY LIFE

Gert had the resources to move around the world as, during the decade I knew him, he was the largest stockholder of Anheuser Busch. He hunted big game in Alaska, had his own horses race at Ascot, lived part-time in Munich, and came to New York each year for the opera season. At times, he asked Beverly Sills what opera she wanted produced; Gert would provide the funding for it.

My introduction to the von Gontards was when their lawyer called Grant Thornton and asked for someone to investigate a potential fraud for one of his clients. I took the assignment, and that began an association that led to a lasting friendship.

The von Gontards created a foundation in the U.S. that financed the production of German theater in America. They wanted me to find out if, as they suspected, the executive director was stealing funds from the foundation. My investigation was inconclusive. Perhaps, I reported, it was a case of sloppy bookkeeping.

I was later amazed when Hildegard (Gert's wife), without notes, grilled the foundation employee about the details of his income and expenses and his lifestyle and its costs. The executive confessed. In exchange for not being turned over to the police, he promised to continue his work with utmost integrity.

After that episode, I met with the von Gontards often when they were in New York. We talked quite a bit, usually over lunch at The Metropolitan Club of New York, where they rented rooms. Over time, I learned the story of Gert's life, and he took an interest in mine, although the hallmarks of each were so vastly different. Gert and Hildegard asked my advice on business and personal matters and, in turn, freely counseled me.

Using his personal stock stored in the cellar of The Metropolitan Club, Gert taught me about wine. When he had tax issues in Germany, I was asked to accompany him to Munich for their resolution. On a free day during that trip, the von Gontards asked their chauffeur to drive me through the beautiful Bavarian Alps in their Rolls Royce auto. Hildegard went so far as to explain the protocol for lunch that day in a high-class mountain restaurant—how to ask the chauffer to join me, the levels of *maître d'* and servers. In Germany, it is Herr Ober and Herr Ober Ober.

Back in New York, Bea and I were the von Gontards' guests at the Metropolitan Opera for a performance of an opera Gert funded. After the last curtain call, the four of us went for dinner at the 21 Club in mid-town. When the doorman saw who was getting out of the limousine, we were asked to wait a moment. I saw why when we entered. All of the staff had formed a line on both sides of an aisle and applauded as we were escorted to Gert's special table. What an experience!

When I asked Gert how I could contact him when he was not in New York, he said that if I left a message at the 21 Club, he would get it. Although I never had the need to test the arrangement, I suspect it would have worked well.

A Multi-talented Man

Hansjorg (Hans) Wyss came to see me in the late 1970s. He had founded and was president of the U.S. division of a Switzerland-based medical device manufacturer that made internal metal plates and screws to fix broken bones. He told me why the Swiss method was superior to the American technique of setting bones and wrapping them in plaster. His plan was to bring the Swiss procedures to the American orthopedic industry.

Hans is about my age. Born in Switzerland, he received a master's degree there in Civil and Structural Engineering. He earned an MBA from Harvard's Graduate School of Business. Before starting the U.S. medical device company, he worked in the textile industry in Pakistan and Turkey and in the steel industry in Belgium.

Hans's business in the United States, Synthes USA, was located in a suburb of Philadelphia. It became Grant Thornton's client, and I directed the accounting and tax services. While the company marketed its products to orthopedic chiefs in U.S. hospitals, it imported from Switzerland the metal plates, screws, and tools required to use them. The U.S. company had to pay for its imports in Swiss francs.

After a while, to avoid the currency exchange costs, Hans opened a U.S. factory to make the products. He was a world-class skier, and it did not come as a surprise that he built the new plant in Colorado.

One day, Hans asked me if I played tennis, and when I said yes, he invited me to play the game with him one morning near his office before business hours. We played several sets. I was happy with the way I competed in the first set, although I lost, 6 to 4. During the second set, I was able to raise my level of play, but again I lost 6 to 4. When Hans asked if I would stay for another set, I did so eagerly. In this last set, I played as well as I ever had—and still lost 6 to 4.

When we had showered and changed back into business clothes, I thanked Hans for the tennis invitation. He thanked me heartily, saying that he was glad to have the opportunity to warm up for the state championship he would be playing in that night.

Hans eventually became Synthes's worldwide CEO and chairman. Our professional relationship was superb. He told me once that, because of my help in his relationship with the Swiss owners of Synthes, he would never stop being a client of Grant Thornton.

In 2012, Hans sold the company for $21.3 billion in cash and stock to Johnson & Johnson. He is reputed to be the wealthiest individual in Switzerland and ranks number 235 on the Bloomberg list of billionaires.

≈ HIGHLIGHTS OF MY LIFE ≈

Photographs

Paul at age 3; Walton Avenue, The Bronx, 1939.

Paul at age 7; with Sylvia; Joyce Kilmer Park, The Bronx, 1943. The Bronx County courthouse is in the background.

PAUL D. NEUWIRTH

Paul at age 11; ready for football with the Midgets, The Bronx, 1947.

Paul at age 17; Camp Seneca, 1953.

≈ HIGHLIGHTS OF MY LIFE ≈

Paul at age 46; in his office, Philadelphia, 1982.

Paul at age 60; studio portrait, 1996.

PAUL D. NEUWIRTH

Paul at age 77; Gulf Shores, AL, going to a Mardi Gras ball, 2013.

Adventures in Scuba Diving

It all started with a visit to the Bahamas, a long time ago. On the beach with nothing to do and bored out of my mind, I took a walk to a nearby strip mall. One shop advertised scuba diving lessons. I was intrigued—I had never tried the sport and knew little about it. The clerk said that they could teach me how to scuba dive in a few days.

"Nothing to it," he reassured me. I signed up.

The scuba shop maintained a huge, above-ground water tank where they taught students like me how to dive and become comfortable with scuba gear. The instructors showed me the equipment and how to use it.

After a while, the instructor said, "I'm going to drop this rock to the tank bottom. I'd like you to dive down, pick it up, and return it to me."

The next thing I knew, I was at the bottom of the tank with the instructor shaking me by the shoulder. He brought me topside and said, "You were falling asleep down there."

"What are you talking about?" I asked. I hadn't remembered a thing.

"It appears you had what we call 'rapture of the deep,'" the instructor told me. The technical term is "nitrogen narcosis." "When you submerge underwater, at a certain depth, you almost lose consciousness. You have to be aware of that. Never go diving without a buddy, and you'll be fine."

I was a little shaken, but I finished the course, including an open-water ocean dive. It was a good experience. I enjoyed doing something new and seeing ocean creatures.

I didn't dive again for a long time. Then, about 20 years ago, I was struck again by the urge to submerge. I took lessons at a pool near my home in Philadelphia. Once again, I had to pass the technical safety exams and demonstrate that I understood how the equipment worked. At last, several weeks later, I had to get into the pool and show that I could handle the equipment under the water.

The final test was an open-water dive. I coupled that with a vacation to the Cayman Islands, where an instructor took me out to the beautiful, blue-green ocean to see if I truly knew how to scuba dive. It was exciting to pass the test and become a "certified" scuba diver.

That was in 1998. I've been scuba diving ever since and have completed more than 60 dives. My log book records my dives at the Bahamas, Grand Cayman, the Dutch Antilles, U.S. Virgin Islands, St. Kitts, Belize, Curacao, Turks and Caicos, Maui, and more. I love it. It's exhilarating to see the world under water. Sometimes, although nobody can hear me, I find myself screaming with joy into my regulator, excited by the thrill of the whole experience.

Because of my comfort in the water, snorkeling is enjoyable, too. On vacation in Israel, Delaney and I snorkeled in the Red Sea. There, in the afternoon, we watched a lionfish, who placidly stared back at us. It's pretty amazing and glorious, I think, that I can still snorkel and scuba dive.

Happily, I've never again experienced the "rapture of the deep." Only once did I decide to go into open water without a buddy—and it was one of the dumbest things I could ever have done. It happened when I was vacationing in Cancun. I was by myself one morning and decided to grab a mask and a snorkel and go off the beach into the ocean. I headed for an area where there weren't a lot of swimmers. I was curious to see if there was anything interesting below the surface.

HIGHLIGHTS OF MY LIFE

I started floating out. I didn't have an air tank, because I was planning to stay near shore. I ended up floating quite far out. There wasn't much to see under the surface, so I looked up to get my bearings. Not only was I far from shore, but the current was against me, and I couldn't easily get back.

Now, I'm a very strong swimmer, but the open ocean can wear out even the best swimmers. I floated, I swam, and it finally dawned on me that I was getting tired and growing weaker by the minute. The shore was still far off, and there was nobody around. I didn't panic, yet.

Fortunately, a fishing boat was tied up nearby where the fishermen were unloading their catch. One of them saw me and he motioned for me to swim to the boat. I did that, but I was too weak to get up the ladder. With a little help, I flopped onto the deck, and stayed there for close to an hour while I regained my strength.

As I said, that was one of the dumbest things I've ever done, but it was the only open-water incident where I had any difficulty. Most of my scuba experience has been marvelous. Underwater has become my special corner of the world.

Air Time

For about 10 years, I worked for a client who owned a peat bog in Michigan. I went there with him to observe his employees count the inventory of paper packaging bags. I really went out to Michigan as a favor. I could have easily enlisted someone else to do it, but this was one of the fellows with whom I truly enjoyed spending time.

When we arrived at the Detroit airport, the client turned to me and said, "Let's find my pilot." I didn't know what he was talking about, but I followed along.

We stopped in front of a small, private plane. My client boarded and the pilot moved over to the copilot seat. I took the seat behind both of them. I asked my client if he had a pilot's license.

"No. If I had a license, I'd be tempted to fly by myself. This way, I always have to be with somebody else," he said. Then he put on a helmet like a welder's mask so he couldn't see anything except the plane's dashboard, and we took off.

That flight was not a good experience for me. I didn't feel safe, because the client was flying blind. Eventually, we got to the bog at Michigan's Upper Peninsula and we landed. He headed off to do his work, and I did mine. I secretly hoped that would be the last of it.

The next day, the small plane returned to pick me up. This time I was in the copilot's seat and the pilot's son was in the back seat. After we took off, the pilot asked me if I would like to fly the airplane.

HIGHLIGHTS OF MY LIFE

I said, "I don't know how to fly."

"It's not hard. If you can steer a car, you can steer the plane." Uh huh. But I was game.

The pilot continued. "You use these pedals to move the tail, and keep your eye on the horizon."

"Okay, what else?" I asked.

"Just do it," the pilot commanded.

So I did it. I found that I got the same feeling as when scuba diving. It was stupendous. We weren't up very high, but the difference in gravity and the difference in motion just blew me away. It was wonderful—until three things happened simultaneously that I felt sure spelled the end for me. On the dashboard, a blue light went on as a buzzer sounded. Then I saw the gauge for the fuel tank was registering empty, just as the pilot reached over to wake up his son.

Close to panic, I asked, "What's happening?"

The pilot answered calmly. "Nothing. Hear that sound? See that blue light? I just installed it, and that's why I woke my son. It lets us know we're approaching Detroit, so we're over a populated area and need to be careful."

"What about the empty fuel gauge?" I asked.

"You don't know this, but we have two fuel tanks. When one empties, the other switches on—and that one is full."

Relieved, I asked, "What happens now? I see the airport."

"Do you see that runway that's right in front of you?" asked the pilot. I said, "Yeah."

"Will you take us down and land us?"

Even though he had a duplicate set of controls that he could engage at any time, that pilot was so trusting! Despite a little turbulence, it all worked out okay.

These experiences have nothing to do with what I did to earn a living. Many of the really exciting moments in my life have come from circumstances that are so outside the realm of what's ordinary for me that adrenaline and stimulation just took over.

Religious Observations

One Passover, I was at Sylvia and Robert's home in Maryland. At the Seder, I sat with Delaney, our three boys, my sister and her two kids, her husband, an assortment of invited friends, and my mother and father. We went through the Seder ritual, and at the end of it, we all sat around, perhaps just a little tipsy from the wine. We were quiet, satisfied, and happy.

When the invited friends had left, I said to my relatives, "I'd like to ask a question, and if you don't want to answer it, just say, 'I'll pass,' no penalty. The question is, 'Do you believe in God? Do you believe in the equivalent of God? Do you believe in a higher power?' It's not a particularly easy question, so do with it as you wish." I was the first to give an answer, and we went around the table.

Stephen was the only one who said, "Yes, I believe, and I can't tell you why. I think that one has to have a special experience that gives you that belief." Then he stopped. He was not a religiously observant person at that time. But he said he believed.

More to the point of the story, as we went around the table, we finally arrived at the patriarch of the family, my father, who had conducted the Seder service. My father could lead a synagogue service from the morning prayers to the evening prayers in Hebrew. He could read the Torah, and was brought up in the orthodox tradition. His was a kosher home, and he observed almost all the holidays, and in his way, acknowledged the Sabbath.

I said, "Pop, your turn. Are you a believer?"

"No, I'm not."

Well, the jaws dropped all around the table, because we all only knew him as an observer. And so I said, "Pop, how come you say you don't believe? You have always been an observer of ritual."

He didn't hesitate. He said, "I'm just hedging my bets."

I said, "Have you ever discussed this with Mom?"

"No."

"Why not?"

He said, "I didn't want your mother calling me a hypocrite."

Then I asked, "Mom, how do you answer the question?"

And she responded, "I know that my mother looks down on me and protects me."

Those were most interesting answers from both of them. Neither answer was what I or anyone else expected. We were all surprised.

I'm not sure how my other sons feel about their religion. Jim is married to a Moroccan woman, who is an observant Orthodox Jew. Years ago, Jim told me, "When Sandra's away, I keep a plate, a fork, a spoon, and a knife in a special drawer. After I take my meals, I wash dishes and the utensils, and I put them back. This way, I don't get mixed up with which dishes are which, and what belongs where." Yet I suspect that over the ensuing years, Jim has become more of an observant believer rather than less.

Richard is a believer, but I think that he believes differently than most people. He worked one summer at the end of high school as assistant to the superintendent of a condominium building down at the Jersey shore. I went to visit him. He stood on the beach looking out over

HIGHLIGHTS OF MY LIFE

the water. He told me then that he sees the planet, this planet, as a living organism, and he believes we are just parts of it. Then he just stopped. I don't know if he has taken that thought further or if he does believe in a higher power. Although I don't know for certain, I think he's not a ritual observer in any traditional way.

I accept whatever ways these boys, now men, have decided to think about life. I owe that to each of them. I think I owe that to most people. And if I didn't accept their views, what difference would it make?

Sometimes I have swallowed hard rather than argue, because these wonderful fellows are the only children I have, and I know that the alternative of estrangement would be a familial disaster.

When I consider religion and other issues, too, I often think about my parents. My father died in 2004 at 103 and my mother two years later, at 97. At their deaths, I did not grieve. I couldn't find a reason for sorrow. They had, on balance, just about what everyone wants. They had long, healthy lives. They had enough of the material things they wanted as well as some of life's intangible pleasures. They were self-made people; they were essentially satisfied. After Mom and Dad's long, healthy lives filled with satisfaction, I couldn't mourn. Instead, I inwardly smiled, because life had been so good for them both. If life is viewed as a kind of game, they were winners.

Real Estate Ventures

Getting into the real estate business was a simple endeavor but, as with many life events, there was a touch of serendipity involved.

Around 1990, Delaney and I were looking to buy a vacation home. We had searched the New Jersey shore, the vacation spot nearest to our home in Philadelphia, but we didn't care for it—too crowded, too close to home.

Then we broadened our horizon and looked at North Carolina, around Duck and Kitty Hawk. We saw some lovely properties, but what we liked, we couldn't afford—and what we could afford, we didn't like. When Delaney's fiftieth birthday was approaching, she said she'd like to spend the day with her parents, who were living in Alabama on the Gulf Coast. I thought it sounded like a fine idea.

Delaney's mother and father lived in a beautiful home on a rise that sloped gently down to a lagoon. They had retired to that part of Alabama after spending their lifetimes in the suburbs of Chicago.

"Well, call your mother and tell her you're coming down," I said.

And she did. Delaney's mother was thrilled that her daughter wanted to spend her birthday in Alabama. She said she would arrange a party and invite all their neighbors.

"What have I done?" Delaney said after hanging up. "I'll be with Mom for a little while and I'll be so full of anxiety that I'll be ready to go home."

I tried to put a positive spin on it. "We've been looking at vacation houses. Why don't you tell your mother that you'd like her to arrange for us to meet a real estate broker? If you get upset with Mom, just tell her you've got an appointment with the real estate broker so you can get out of the house."

It turns out that Delaney had nothing to worry about. We had a wonderful time with her mother and father and all their neighbors and friends. It was a beautiful birthday for her.

During our visit, I looked at local real estate on my own. While I knew nothing about Alabama land or houses, I felt that something big was about to happen. I didn't know what, but I had the feeling that a lot of action was taking place. After we got home, I said to Delaney, "Let's buy something on the Gulf Coast." I saw it more as an investment rather than a vacation home.

It turned out that purchasing real estate in Alabama was a good thing to do at that time. You could take a rock, throw it, and buy whatever it landed on. The next day or very soon after, you could resell that same piece of property at a better price. At least, that's how it seemed to me.

We returned to Alabama with a real estate-purchasing agenda. I picked out some vacant lots on Ono Island, wrote down the names of the owners or realtors, and returned to Philadelphia and made some phone calls. Seeing myself as a big city slicker, I offered each rural seller less than the asking price. Some said no and some just hung up the phone.

After a half-dozen rejections, exasperated, I called Tom, our Gulf Shores realtor. "Just buy any lot in the group you have shown us," I said. "You pick out the lot. I don't care what price you pay. Just buy it." He did, paying the asking price, and we were in the game.

A short while after our first Alabama land purchase, Tom called me to say that a new high-rise condominium was being built right on the

Gulf of Mexico beach. He explained why we should buy a unit in it, who the builder was, and why it was likely to be a success.

I asked Tom to send me the purchase documents, saying that I would read them and get back to him with a decision.

"No," our realtor responded. "The units are selling quickly. If you want one, send me a check today." I did.

Naively, I had blindly—without significant investigation—bought a beachfront condominium unit. I hadn't even read the purchase contract. I'd relied on nothing but trust in my business instinct and in Tom's honesty, a sense of adventure, and lots of luck. It was a successful investment.

I was hooked.

After our first investing episodes, over the ensuing years, we bought and sold thirty or so pieces of property on the Gulf Coast. We had a lot of fun doing it. We bought undeveloped land, condominium units, and a couple of single-family houses. Our transactions primarily were in south Baldwin County in the towns of Gulf Shores and Orange Beach.

Suddenly, we were in the rental business, too. Sometimes we would use one of the condo units at the beach for ourselves. And we ended up buying a vacation home, completing the task that had started our adventure in real estate. We still use our house in Gulf Shores for winter vacations. It was a delight when family members visited us. My mother and father stayed with us once and were all smiles. I think that our vacations at the beach reminded them of their early years at New York beaches.

When Delaney's mother died and her father was alone, he would visit while we were in town. When we owned condominiums on the water, he would stop by. When we had to evacuate our home because hurricanes were coming, we would go to the assisted living facility where he stayed. We would just come in unannounced and he'd put us up. We were lucky to have such a wonderful relationship with him.

I never bet the farm on any of our investments. In some instances, I partnered with Dr. George Popky, who also enjoyed the adventure. A few times, Richard invested with us as a partner. It is always a thrill for me to be in an investment venture with Rich.

In a way, the real estate game is for me somewhat like gambling in a casino—with a longer run for our money. There is a similar excitement in owning a winning piece of property. When we had losing properties—and there were some—I felt I could afford to sustain the loss.

Despite the recession of 2008, we're still in the real estate business. Prices dropped precipitously during that recession, and I still own properties that are financially under water. Mostly, we did well economically, even as we weathered the 2007–2008 severe down-turn in real estate.

The circumstances were almost always enjoyable and sometimes unusual. One year, with Dr. Popky, I bought a condominium in mid-June. Wanting to get renters in for the week of the Fourth of July holiday, I hired Lucy, a decorator, to work her magic. She was able to fix up the unit so it could be rented for the holiday. She told me later that everything worked out very well, except when it came to bringing in a convertible sofa. It wouldn't fit in the elevator. She told me that her helpers lowered the elevator, moved the sofa on top of the elevator, and raised the lift to the tenth floor. Then they took the sofa out and moved it into our unit. She's a clever and daring lady.

When we bought our vacation home at the Peninsula Golf and Racquet Club in Gulf Shores, it was the model home for a new community section. It was about one-third furnished. We again hired Lucy.

"Well, what do you want me to do?" she asked after checking out the home.

I said, "Finish decorating in the same style that you see has been started by the builder." I said, "When you are finished, I don't want to have to bring anything with me but a toothbrush, and our house should be ready for us."

That's what Lucy did. Today, our home at The Peninsula is furnished seamlessly. Delaney and I have been working with this interior designer for the better part of a quarter century, always with superior results.

During almost 30 years, we've had good fortune with renters—all except for one. After I bought a small, vacant, single-family house in Orange Beach, I asked our real estate broker for help in finding a tenant. We rented the house to a man who, our broker told us, had been recommended by his church. A church endorsement counts for something positive, I thought.

Soon thereafter, I received a call in Philadelphia from somebody in that area of Alabama who described the house and asked if it was mine. "Yes," I said.

The caller went on, "I think you might want to know that the police are outside and it looks like they're arresting whoever is living there."

It turns out we had rented to a drug dealer—the kind who kept pit bulls chained up on the porch. The inside of our house was beaten up badly. Our tenant exited abruptly with the police and we never saw or heard from him again. But that was a singular event. In most cases, our rental agents run background checks on potential tenants. On the whole, it's worked out well.

Early one morning, Delaney and I went for a walk on the beach in Orange Beach, Alabama. We saw a person far down the beach walking toward us. As we approached each other, we saw that this man, in his thirties, had on his shoulder a grey parrot. Of course, we stopped to talk with the beach walker, who told us how he lets the parrot fly free at the beach and that it always returns to his shoulder.

We listened to a summary of the natural science of grey parrots with emphasis on their high intelligence. When we heard that our new beach friend lives in Huntsville, Alabama, and works for NASA, we decided that it is the parrot that is the mathematical engineer for NASA's space flights.

I've been asked whether I would encourage my children and grandchildren to get into buying, selling, and renting real estate. I would tell them to do what makes them happy. There are few things better than enjoying one's work.

Freud said, "The only two things that matter are work and love." If you've got both, you're way ahead of the game.

The world has forever engaged in buying and selling. Transactions in real estate can be one's work or a hobby. I would advise, "If that's what you'd like to do, go for it."

The World's Fair

When I was four years old, it was a singular time in my life. I probably bear some of the scars from that time that still twitch in a cold rain. But there were wondrous times, too.

I recall one day with great clarity. I was four years old, and my father had taken me to the 1939–1940 World's Fair in Flushing Meadows, Queens. I remember so clearly that Dad showed me the General Motors exhibit called "Futurama" in the 36,000-square-foot "Highways and Horizons" pavilion.

"Futurama" was the fair's most popular exhibit. It was designed by Norman Bel Geddes and presented a model of what GM thought city infrastructure would look like 20 years later. It featured automated highways and huge suburban developments.

Visitors to the exhibit sat in moving chair-cars. Each seat had its own sound system, and the chairs moved on a fixed track around a huge, extensive diorama of the City of the Future. The chairs themselves, attached next to each other, rose over 20 feet in the air—at age four, of course, I had never experienced anything like it.

"Futurama" displayed things few people had seen before: fluorescent street lights, clover-leaf highways that passed over and around one another, and automobiles that looked like they could drive in either direction. "Futurama" was massive, too, with more than 500,000 individually designed, tiny model homes, one million little trees representing 18 different species, and 50,000 scale-size cars. Bridges, rivers, cities, lakes, and forests completed this vision of the future.

GM's designers had said, "This is what a city will look like in the 1960s"—and they were mostly right!

I remember also visiting a Borden's Dairy Farm exhibit showcasing Elsie the Cow. She was being milked using an electric milking machine. That blew my city-kid mind.

The symbol for the World's Fair was a pair of structures called the Trylon and Perisphere. Neither of these modernistic buildings exist today. The Trylon was a pointy monolith more than 600 feet high. At ground level, it was connected to the Perisphere by what was, at the time, the world's longest escalator. The Perisphere looked like a massive golf ball.

I remember walking in front of the Perisphere, talking with my father about how nice it looked. All of a sudden, a window opened on the side of this round object, and the face of a man appeared in the window. Because I had no idea what was happening or why, I became terrified. But Dad reassured me.

I came home from the fair with two souvenirs: a Heinz pickle pin and a cane. The cane is inscribed with "World's Fair, 1939."

I don't have that pin anymore, but I did find a replacement when I was an adult. The visit to the World's Fair must have impressed me mightily. In my later years, I started finding postcards from the fair at flea markets and antique stores, and I started a collection. I particularly like the cards with pictures of the General Motors exhibit, the Borden Dairy Farm, and the Trylon and Perisphere.

E.L. Doctorow's novel *World's Fair* reminded me of my experience there. I identify with the main character—a boy growing up in the

Bronx, in an apartment just a few blocks east of the Grand Concourse. Through various circumstances, the family moves to a new apartment on the Grand Concourse. His apartment is on one side, and on the other there's an empty lot on which a new school is being built.

I actually attended that school, a junior high school, described in the book. Doctorow beautifully portrays the general area where I grew up. What a treat it was to read.

A Big Book Needs an Editor

In the mid-1980s, when I was about 50 years old and working and living in Philadelphia, I was contacted by an editor at McGraw Hill Companies, the large book publisher. He asked if I would be interested in editing a book about auditing that was going into its second edition.

Since my professional work was connected with auditing and I was teaching university students about auditing, I wanted to know more. I learned that the first edition of *Handbook for Auditors* was a well-known volume with chapters by various authors. It had been edited in 1971 by James A. Cashin when he was in his seventies. By the time the McGraw Hill editor found me, Cashin was nearing 85 years old and didn't want to work on a second edition.

With great excitement, I said, "Yes, I'll do it!"

I asked one of my accounting firm colleagues, John Levy, if he would collaborate with me on the book. John accepted, and together we edited the second edition of the work, retitled *Cashin's Handbook for Auditors*. We asked many practicing CPAs to each write a chapter. John and I read and edited their manuscripts—roughly 700 pages dedicated to the craft and science of auditing.

Our new edition was updated to cover the newest, generally accepted professional auditing standards, norms, techniques, and ethical codes. Our book was enriched with the experience of the authors of each chapter.

During the process, I visited Mr. Cashin at his home in Sarasota, Florida, where we discussed the second edition. It was important to him and to me that he was satisfied that his name—with my name, and John Levy's—would be on a new work of value.

It took us about a year to complete the manuscript for the second edition. Finally, when the new book was published, the reviews in professional journals were good. It was gratifying that the work was well-received. The new book became a text adopted by teachers of auditing in colleges and universities around the world. I was surprised and thrilled when the book was translated into Spanish and was used in countries in South America.

The profession of auditing is dynamic. Changes in standards and in methodology are ongoing. Time takes its toll, and the book eventually became obsolete. But for about a decade, it was considered a book for auditors to have in their library and as a desk reference. I'm very proud of that.

Sometimes I take a copy of the book off my shelf and flip to the rear dust jacket—I look so young in that photograph! From time to time, I still receive a royalty check from McGraw Hill. It's now not more than a couple of dollars, but it reminds me of the satisfying work I did 30 years ago.

Stamp Collecting Opens the World

Stamp collecting ranks high among the activities that I very much enjoyed as a youngster. When I was ten or eleven, my father gave me an international stamp album with places to put stamps from countries around the world. He probably also gave me a package of used stamps. That started me on my way in a wonderful hobby and a pursuit that painlessly made me smarter about both our country and the countries beyond our borders.

Collecting stamps was satisfying in a number of ways. I could work on my collection when I wanted to, quietly, by myself. I learned that there were companies that would mail me stamps for sale, mounted in small books, "on approval." Each stamp had a price, often between one cent and 50 cents. I could take the stamps that I wanted and that I could afford and send back the rest, along with the money for those I bought. There was a quiet excitement in seeing the pages in my album filling up with stamps. I enjoyed finding all the stamps of a set; that is, different denominations of the same picture or of related scenes.

Stamps most likely led to my first exposure to countries in Africa. Some of the African countries issued stamps that were larger than U.S. stamps and showed pictures of a kind not found on American issues.

Often, they had pictures of Africans in outdoor activities or of animals native to that continent.

It is from stamps that I first learned about inflation. Many older German stamps were overprinted in large, black numbers during World War II to show their new values, due to the dramatic German inflation.

European countries became more real to me as I learned the difference between the names Suisse (Switzerland) and Sverge (Sweden) printed on each country's stamps. Some stamps were issued in the shape of triangles. On the rare days when I acquired a triangular stamp, it became a highlight of my collection.

Of all my neighborhood friends, only one— my best friend, Michael—also collected stamps. Sometimes, we would compare our collections and trade our duplicates. Some of my fifth- and sixth-grade classmates also were collectors, and I traded with them, too.

Trading stamps has some of the same attributes as a business activity. Each party wants to give up stamps with about the same value as those they receive. Thinking back on it now, from the vantage point of many later decades, I am still embarrassed remembering the few trades when I gave up much more than I got.

When I was old enough to go by myself from the Bronx to mid-Manhattan, via the subway, I felt it was a mark of growing up. Sometimes on those excursions, I went to Gimbels department store because it had a very good stamp department. Jacques Minkus operated the stamp department for more than 50 years, and he is often credited with bringing stamp collecting to the masses as a hobby. It also didn't hurt that our president, Franklin D. Roosevelt, was a renowned stamp collector.

At Gimbels top-of-the-line stamp department, I could look through vast collections of stamps and albums. My visits there opened up for me what was possible in the world of stamp collecting. I learned about the Dumont Stamp Shop on Sixth Avenue, a stand-alone stamp collectors' store. Even without much money, I could buy stamps for two cents or four cents.

Every Sunday, when I would go to buy *The New York Times* for Mom and Dad, I looked forward to the newspaper's section dedicated to stamps and stamp collecting. Also in this section were many very small classified ads, posted by individuals or companies selling stamps. That's where I learned about buying stamps on approval.

Delaney and I each were surprised to learn that we both—of course, unknown to each other—had collected stamps during the same years. We had each kept our childhood collections.

Today, "the hobby of kings and the king of hobbies" remains quite popular—more than five million Americans collect stamps—although the Internet has drastically changed how everyone pursues their hobbies. Gimbels closed in 1987 and the Dumont Stamp Shop is gone. For those who want to explore "stamps on approval," that business model lives on at the Mystic Stamp Company, the Littleton Coin Company, and others.

Always Skating

Many activities of my childhood fall under the broad category of "skating." Beginning around age ten or eleven, my friends and I all enjoyed roller skating. The skates, each with four wheels, were made of metal and were worn clamped to street shoes. Each skate had a leather strap that tied around the ankle and a set of metal grips that tightened on either side of the front of shoes.

We skated on city sidewalks, but it was much more satisfying to roll on the smooth macadam street gutters where the cars drove. No autos were produced during World War II, and few were made in the several years just after the war. Skating in the street was not much of a safety issue.

In the neighborhood where I grew up, some blocks were not suitable to build apartment houses because they were right next to the continual noise of the elevated subway. While developers could have easily put up residential buildings there, nobody would have moved into them. Instead, land owners built tennis courts there, although few tennis players showed up in the summer. In the winter, when it was too cold to play, the nets were taken down and the courts were flooded until they froze and turned into ice skating rinks.

My father bought me a pair of hockey ice skates. So that I wouldn't outgrow them right away, he purchased them several sizes too large.

We put a cloth inside the shoes, in front of my toes, to take up the extra space. I used the same pair for years.

My mother did a wonderful thing for me: She took me to Madison Square Garden, which was then on 50th Street and Eighth Avenue in Manhattan. It had an ice skating rink that may have been where the professional hockey teams played when they were in town. When the Rangers' games were not scheduled, the ice rink was open to the public.

The Garden had some employees who gave ice skating lessons, and that is where I learned the essentials. Mom occasionally also took me to Rockefeller Center, and I also had lessons at that famous outdoor ice skating rink. Back then, it wasn't too crowded to skate at this major midtown tourist attraction.

When Delaney and I first got together, around 1983, we spent a long weekend at the Pocono Manor Inn hotel in Pennsylvania's Pocono Mountains. It was wintertime, and we decided to ice skate. I knew that Delaney, a Midwestern girl, knew how to skate. She had her skates with her. I probably rented a pair from the hotel.

We were just going back and forth on the frozen lake when Delaney asked if I wanted to race with her just once around the lake. I said, "Sure," and we took off. I chased but found that I couldn't catch her. Every time I got close, Delaney pulled away.

After one circuit, she asked, "Do you want to do it again?" I said, "Okay." On the third try, now with my male ego at stake, I put everything I had into the race and again almost caught her, but couldn't quite make it.

Hardest to swallow was that, all this time, Delaney was skating backwards.

I first used in-line skates on a July Fourth holiday when I was close to age 60. Over the holiday weekend, a company that rented and sold the skates came into our neighborhood offering to lend a pair to anyone who wanted to try them.

I took off my shoes, stepped into a pair the new-style skates, and tried to move along the street. Although I moved unsteadily and had to go very slowly, I liked both the idea and feeling of this new sport. After two or three blocks, my love of street skating was reborn.

For about 15 years after that, Delaney and I went in-line skating every chance we had. Philadelphia's Fairmont Park has beautiful, scenic paths for biking, running, or skating. We took our skates (it wasn't long before I bought my own equipment) and skated whenever we could—on weekends, holidays, and whenever we had free days during the week. Over time, I became a reasonably good skater. I looked forward to the exhilaration I felt at each outing on skates.

We took our skates with us when we attended a wedding on Nantucket and soared on the island's narrow, hilly paths. Several times, I found myself careening downhill, screaming from fright. How we didn't fall, I don't know. We conquered our fears and skated with reckless abandon—just that once. That was more than enough.

One day, back in Philadelphia on our usual skating route in Fairmount Park, I was coming down a relatively steep hill on one of the bike paths. With in-line skates, although you can brake to slow, it's not easy to stop if you are on an incline. As I came down the hill, I saw at the bottom a group of a half dozen young teenage boys with their bicycles. They were doing what young teenage boys do—standing and talking to each other. They were right in the middle of the path.

I knew I couldn't stop. I had to quickly make a choice: either skate right into this group of kids, with the mayhem that would result, or veer off the concrete path and onto the surrounding grass, where the skate wheels would catch in the earth and stop turning. To avoid the boys, I chose the grass.

As I rolled by them, the kids remained oblivious. I was wearing all the right stuff on my wrists, elbows, and knees, and I wore a helmet. But of course, I fell—and when you hit your head, you hit your head.

I soon realized that I needed help. I was taken to the emergency room at the Medical College of Pennsylvania, which was just a short distance from where I had been skating. Coincidentally, I was a member of the hospital's board of directors. I was quickly informed that I had a concussion. My medical treatment was magnificent, for which I am grateful.

After the concussion healed, I went back to skating—very carefully. Delaney and I both stopped skating about five years ago. I didn't feel comfortable doing it anymore, and I worried about the danger of getting a more serious injury. Yet, in the decade and a half that we skated in all seasons, skating was a joy for us.

Building Scooters

If a young teenage fellow today wants a Razor brand scooter, he'll likely go to a bicycle store to get one. When my friends and I were age 14 or so, we didn't do that; instead, we made our own scooters.

We'd ask the local fruit and vegetable store owner for empty wooden crates that the produce came in. The storekeeper usually agreed, as he would otherwise just throw them away as trash.

We usually used one crate for the scooter body and a second crate for parts. We stood a crate upright. Then, from the second crate, we'd take a long slat from its side and nail it to the bottom of the upright crate so that it stuck out behind, creating the board to stand on. We'd also create handle bars by removing the sturdy edges from one end of the second crate and nailing them to the top of the upright crate so they stuck out a bit.

Next, we took apart a metal roller skate so that it became two pieces, each with two wheels. We would nail one half of the skate to the underside of the back of the slat we'd made to stand on, and nail the other half to the underside of the front. Voila! We had a scooter.

Surprisingly, these scooters worked and lasted. When they broke, we took them apart and built new ones. Although it took some ingenuity, the construction was relatively easy to do. It was satisfying to build a scooter— satisfying that it worked, and satisfying that we could do it ourselves.

Goodbye Walton Avenue

My parents and I lived in an apartment on Walton Avenue until I was about 15 years old. Then our family moved one block west to a larger apartment in a newer building on the Grand Concourse.

I got married when I was 21—young by today's standards, but totally normal for the 1950's—and moved to Yonkers, NY, to a garden apartment near The Adventurers, a fast-food and hot dog stand on Central Avenue.

My parents too left the Bronx in the early 1960s when, like so many others in the neighborhood, they were motivated by a rapidly changing population and altering character of the area. Mom and Dad moved to 69th Street and Second Avenue in Manhattan, where they rented an apartment in a high rise. They lived there for the rest of their lives.

The story of the Bronx residents from the 1930s through today can be told largely by demographics. In the early decades, a large segment of New York City's Jewish population, mostly the children of Jewish immigrants, was starting to do well economically. Coming out of the Lower East Side of Manhattan, but unable to afford the cost of mid-Manhattan housing, many made the same decision: to move to the Bronx, right to that neighborhood where I was born and grew up. The top attractions of the Bronx were lower housing costs and swift transportation to Manhattan by any of three subway lines.

There were few changes in the population of the Bronx through and right after the World War Two years. Then, in the late 1950s and early 1960s, the comparatively affordable housing in the Bronx attracted a new population of African Americans and Hispanics. Over the last decades through today, a more diversified group has taken up residence in the Bronx. An economic revival is underway bringing with it infrastructure improvements, significant drops in crime rates and a return to stability.

More About Mom

I only knew her as Ann. Mom was born Annie, and from time to time, she later called herself Anna.

Annie's childhood was impoverished. She left school at age sixteen for full-time work to help support her family. Mom seldom talked to me about her early life or the years leading up to her marriage. Rather than dwell on the past or regret what was or could have been, the Ann I knew always looked forward.

It seemed to me that my mother was much like the other mothers in the neighborhood. It was only much later, when Mom was in her eighties and early nineties, that I learned of the issues of her life. She wrote her autobiography, telling "the truth" as she knew it. She gave me the finished manuscript, written longhand in pencil, which I published in a small edition.

Only when I read her story did I fully focus on and understand her intelligence, striving, and strength. I wish I had known her life story much earlier in my own life, so that I could have recognized the full dimensions of this singular woman.

Mom was a caring and loving mother. In all my growing-up years, I never was in want of any material things. Mom made sure that her young son was always clean. Our apartments were always clean, too. In every season, I had whatever clothes I needed.

Mom was the point person in our family. She took meal time seriously, determining menus, buying the ingredients, and doing the cooking. My mouth waters as I remember Mom's tasty cooking. I recall only one cookbook in the kitchen: Mom taught herself how and what to cook from *The Settlement Cook Book*. In our kosher home, the meals were healthy and balanced with meat, poultry, vegetables, and fruit predominating. Even during World War II, when food was rationed, our table was always full. I think this was due, in part, to Mom's cordial relationships with the local grocer, kosher butcher, and fruit and vegetable vendor.

Meal times were good times because, when Mom and Dad, Sylvia, and I sat around the table, conversation was never lacking. Usually, Mom or Dad started talking about current events, politics, business, or any issue of interest to them. Often, Mom and Dad held different opinions. The wonderful characteristic of these discussions was that my sister and I could participate, and we were encouraged to do so. We could say what we thought and felt. We were treated as equal contributors. Our views counted, and we did not have to accept what our parents said if we disagreed.

Yes, Mom was a housewife, but that was not the end of her story. She was interested in the world around her and beyond. Although she'd had no formal schooling after age 16, she was interested in the arts, especially painting and music. Ann took oil painting lessons. She came home one day carrying her easel and paint box and a painting she made showing the statue of Columbus at Columbus Circle at 59th Street in Manhattan. She had spent most of the day in her smock and cap, creating the painting while autos and pedestrians whizzed all around her. She was undaunted, and the painting was pretty good.

Mom loved to sing. She joined a chorus to sing oratorios at the 92nd Street YM-YWHA where, on her own, she went to rehearsals and recitals. Ann made sure that her interest in the arts was imparted to me.

HIGHLIGHTS OF MY LIFE

For that, I am grateful. Mom went with me to New York's Metropolitan Museum of Art to show me the exhibits. She let each exhibit speak to me for itself, whether it was the magnificent Arms and Armor collection or the world-renowned Van Gogh paintings. I grew up with reproductions of paintings from the Met on the wall above my bed.

Mom registered me for attendance at the Young People's Concerts at Carnegie Hall where Leonard Bernstein and the New York Philharmonic Orchestra introduced the audience to classical music.

In her autobiography, Ann explained that she had taken piano lessons as a child, although there was little or no money to pay for them and the only piano she could use was at her teacher's home. When I was a young teen, Mom and Dad bought a piano. That day, Mom wrote, was of great significance to her. Now I can imagine why.

Almost immediately, she asked a local piano teacher to help her relearn how to play the instrument. Mom arranged for Sylvia and me to have piano lessons, too. It was one of the finest things that Mom did for us. Although my musical ear is far from flawless, what has been perfect is my enjoyment of playing the piano. The piano that Mom and Dad bought is now in my home in Philadelphia. It is played only rarely now, but it reminds me of how Mom passed her love of music to me.

One day in childhood, I casually said that I'd like to learn to play the guitar. It wasn't long after that Mom bought the instrument for me and arranged for weekly guitar lessons. It is wonderful that I can trace, almost in a straight line, the emotional hold that music had on Mom, and has on me—and now on Steve, Jim, and Rich, as well as on the grandchildren. Musical talent and showmanship may be expressing itself at its height in our grandchildren.

It was always a treat when Mom went to the movies with me. We both enjoyed going to the Ascot Theater, near Fordham Road, to see

British films, especially those with Alec Guinness. That was when I was in my teens. The very first movies Mom took me to had less benign outcomes.

When I was five years old, we saw *Pinocchio,* and a year or so later, *Lassie Come Home,* both Walt Disney studio films. The former upset me, as the hero was separated from his "father," and the latter had me crying when the boy and his dog, separated by a fence, couldn't get to each other. Sometimes a mother's best intentions produce unintended consequences, but this happened rarely with Mom.

Although Ann was accepted by her neighbors, friends, and acquaintances as a highly educated woman, she had gone through most of her life without a high school diploma. Mom felt somewhat incomplete. In her fifties, she set out to relieve the ache. Mom studied for and passed New York's GED exam. It was a happy day when she knocked on the apartment door in Riverdale and, without a word, handed me an envelope that contained her high school equivalency degree.

Almost immediately, Mom enrolled at Hunter College, taking courses in subjects as diverse as Shakespeare and Spanish. When asked what she liked best about college, Mom said very quickly, "Being with the young people."

The Games We Played

Nobody had made an announcement, and it wasn't on anyone's calendar. Yet my friends and I knew, without being told, that a certain day each spring marked the beginning of Marble Season—time to bring our marbles outside. Every day, for a week or two, we challenged each other in games in which the winner's marble collection grew and the loser went home with fewer and fewer of the little glass orbs.

The local grocery stores stocked Philadelphia cream cheese that came packaged in wooden boxes about a foot long by three inches wide. The nearby grocer gave me an empty box each spring, and I cut small, marble-size holes along its length. I set the box against the street curb and let the neighborhood kids roll their marbles toward the box. If the marble went in a hole, the player won three marbles. If the marble missed a hole, I kept it. On most days, I went home with more marbles than I started with.

Somehow, without formal communication, we also just knew when it was baseball card season. This was the time to go outside with the cards we had collected from packages of bubble gum. One game we played was to spin cards toward the wall of an apartment building; the boy whose card was closest to the wall won and took the losing cards. Another game was for one player to flip his card to the sidewalk. The second player did the same, trying to match the first card, either picture up or down. Years later, some of the baseball cards had real value to collectors—but as young teens, we were interested only in how many cards we accumulated.

Kids in my neighborhood played a sidewalk game that was not unique to New York City. It was played in cities throughout the country, mostly by girls, although the boys tried it from time to time. Kids used chalk to draw a diagram on the sidewalk of boxes each with a number—one through eight.

A skate key (the tool we used to tighten the clamps of metal skates that attached them to our shoes) was tossed into the numbered boxes in the order that the game called for. The player hopped in each box and retrieved the skate key. All over the country, the game was called "hopscotch." Uniquely, in the Bronx it was called "potsy."

Many years later, when I was married and with children, I moved to Riverdale, the highest elevation of land in New York City and still part of the Bronx. A couple of my new friends asked if I want to play tennis with them. I agreed, but once on the court, I was embarrassed by how badly I played. I needed so much help with my game that I hired a pro to teach me. The pro was an African American man who, because of the age we lived in, had missed the window that would have allowed him to participate in big time professional tennis. His skill was outstanding. I can only imagine what he'd been like when he was a few years younger.

The pro taught me on outdoor public courts in the Bronx. We also played on indoor courts with slick, concrete floors in a Manhattan armory. At the end of each lesson, we played a game with a rule that, if I scored a point, he would buy me an ice cream soda. In the couple of years we played the end-of-lesson game, I never got the soda. But I always went home happy and, over time, my game became much better.

≋ HIGHLIGHTS OF MY LIFE ≋

When I moved to Philadelphia, I joined a country club where, on weekends, I continued playing tennis. In those years, I could hold my own on a tennis court, but "club hacker" was probably the operative description.

Later in my life, Delaney and I bought a vacation home in Gulf Shores, Alabama. We are in a community that's built on three nine-hole golf courses and also has eight magnificent, Har-Tru tennis courts that get a lot of use. The courts are manicured and rolled every day. For the last five years, I have played on these courts, often with a pro. The joy the game has brought me is immeasurable. I am a better player now than at any time in my life. Now, at the beginning of my eighth decade, I am exhilarated almost every time I walk onto a tennis court.

When I lived in Wynnewood, Pennsylvania, my neighbor and good friend Ellis and I played tennis singles once a week for several years at a nearby, indoor tennis club. By happenstance, my locker was right next to the locker of the professional basketball player Charles Barkley. At that time, Barkley had an apartment near the tennis facility in the western suburbs of Philadelphia. When he was in town, he would come to that tennis club, but not to play tennis—he would come to soak in the hot tub. Although I am six feet tall, Barkley is such a tall and wide man that, if he was changing his clothes while I stood behind him, you wouldn't even see me. Barkley is so big that, next to him, I seemed to disappear.

The only other time I had that same experience was one day in New York when I went out for a midday lunch break on Sixth Avenue and 45th Street. Muhammad Ali was coming down the street. He was very gracious to the crowd, but as I fell in behind him, I realized I could not see what was happening beyond him. He didn't quite blot out the sun, but at six feet three inches, he appeared as a huge figure.

Meeting sports professionals happened to Jim the year he turned eight. We were living in Riverdale at the time and Jim was fascinated with the game of basketball. He was very good at it for someone that age. He loved it so much that, at bedtime, he often would go to sleep with a basketball wrapped in his arms. Jim embraced the sport.

That year, as part of his birthday present, we went to Madison Square Garden to see the Knicks play. We had nice but not special seats. One of the ushers came by and asked me if he could borrow my son Jim for the halftime show.

I asked, "What for?"

The usher said, "They'll take him out on the floor, and he'll be fine, and then we'll bring him back."

I asked Jim if that was okay, and he said, "Sure."

The usher took Jim away. As promised, at halftime, Jim was brought out to the basketball floor together with one of the players—we don't know which one—who was dressed as Santa Claus, complete with false beard and red costume. Silently, using pantomime signals, "Santa Claus" directed Jim on what to do with the basketball. Jim surprised the player because he could do whatever Santa asked of him.

"Do a layup up close," Santa instructed, and Jim put the ball in the basket. Then they moved to the foul line, and Jim again put the ball in the basket. They moved around for a while, and then Jim really got into it. When Santa Claus moved him back to the top of the key and said, "Shoot from here," Jim just shook his head, moved a little closer, and put the ball in the hoop.

The crowd showed how much it enjoyed this performance by applauding. As halftime ended, and the Knicks and the other team came back on the court to warm up, Santa Claus brought Jim to the Knicks and introduced him to the players. Walt Frazier talked to Jim and even put his arms around him and massaged his neck, adding to Jim's wonderful and surprising birthday present.

HIGHLIGHTS OF MY LIFE

When we lived in Wynnewood, Pennsylvania, I played basketball games with our three boys using the backboard and hoop at the end of our driveway. We also spent time playing tennis. When the boys, as youngsters, got on the courts with me, they did not think that they could keep up with my game, and so they didn't—until a singular day in 1977.

Jim, who was then in high school, was playing tennis with me. He saw that I couldn't return a couple of shots that he hit. A special look of understanding crossed his face when he realized he had figured out how to beat me. From then on, I was never again able to win when I played Jim.

In my opinion, the day your son can beat you at a sport brings one of the greatest joys of fatherhood.

One of the most outstanding tennis matches of my life was with Stephen. He invited Delaney and me to the White House for lunch and tennis. (Writing the last sentence brings back the thrill of that day.) At the time, Steve was serving as Associate White House Counsel to President Clinton. His office was right next to the president's! It was an awesome experience for me to play tennis with Steve in the shadow of the White House. When I looked up between serves, I could see the Secret Service walking with their machine guns along the White House roof.

I don't know how it may be now, but at that time, the tennis court was in a secluded part of the grounds of the White House. From outside the fence around the grounds, nobody could see the court or players. I was grateful to Stephen for inviting me to play and to see his new office. I felt overwhelmed, then and now, with thoughts of how a member of our family had made it next to the most powerful place and person on the planet.

I thought about the family line from my grandfather, Sam the tailor, to his son, my father, the CPA—and then me, and then Stephen, who was advising the president of the United States. The imagery, for me, is so powerful: An immigrant comes to New York and carves out his niche with the hopes that his progeny will flourish, and then they do. It is a fabulous example of what a great country we live in. Indeed, we are in a land of opportunity.

I recall the day that Bill Clinton took over the White House. The prior administration was finished. It had moved out, and Clinton and his people were moving in. Stephen put my name and Delaney's on the list of those who would be allowed to enter the White House that day. We waited for our names to be called and then we went inside.

Stephen showed where his office was going to be. Pictures of George H. W. Bush were being taken off the walls. Drapes were coming down and pictures of the new president were being put up. It was one of the highlights of my life, for two reasons. One, the experience of being at that time in that place was unique and awesome; and two, our son was where he was. It was an overpowering feeling that remains with me to this day.

When Delaney and I visited Stephen at the White House another time, it was a wonderful experience in its entirety, but this visit required a different entry procedure. Steve had submitted our names to the guest list and we were cleared to enter. But when it was my turn to walk through the metal detector, it started to buzz.

Alerted, the security people wanted to know what I was carrying that set off the alarm, but I wasn't carrying anything.

I went through again. Same result.

They put me through a third time.

Finally, somebody asked, "Have you had a medical test for your heart recently?"

"Yes," I replied. "I had what's called a nuclear stress test."

HIGHLIGHTS OF MY LIFE

Those seemed to be the magic words. "Okay, the radioactive chemicals that went into your body so that the pictures could be read easily are setting off our machine."

With the mystery solved, we passed through and spent our time with Stephen. Being with him next to the highest seat of power on earth was as marvelous as you can imagine. Later in the day, we went from the West Wing to the East Wing and had to pass through another metal detector. This time, when the security people knew my name, they said, "You're the nuclear guy," and they let me pass right through.

Revisiting Roots

In the fall of 2016, after driving on Jerome Avenue in the Bronx, our son Jim called to ask, "Dad is this where you grew up?" I explained the outlines of the neighborhood where I spent all those years of my childhood. Jim asked if I would go back to the Bronx with him and show him the details of those places.

A few Sundays after that, I took Amtrak from Philadelphia to New York's Penn Station, where Jim and his 15-year-old son, Russell, were waiting. We drove up the West Side Highway, across 155th Street, and over the Macomb's Dam Bridge to Jerome Avenue, near Yankee Stadium. At 165th Street, Jim drove up to Walton Avenue. After Jim parked, we walked the area.

First, a little backstory: About 30 years prior, in the 1980s, my sister Sylvia and I realized that we both had recurring dreams about the streets in the Bronx where we grew from children into young adults. We both felt compelled to go back and see the neighborhood, and together, we did. At that that time, the Bronx was a different and intimidating place.

The middle-class Jewish population of our time had moved away and had been replaced by a population composed almost entirely of African Americans and Hispanics. The old, very safe neighborhood had become one of New York City's highest crime areas. You could almost feel it. The apartment building front doors had heavy locks. The streets were strewn with trash.

Sylvia and I went into Joyce Kilmer Park, about a half block from the apartment building we had lived in. We were disturbed by what we saw. The park had a statue and a fountain, called Lorelei Fountain—also sometimes called Heinrich Heine Fountain—which had been a fixture of our youth. We'd tell our friends, "I'll meet you at the fountain," or, "I'll meet you at the statue." We felt heartbroken when we saw both the Lorelei Fountain and the statue broken, defaced, and covered with graffiti.

The park itself, a major play area of our childhood, was no longer an inviting spot. It seemed dirty and dangerous.

Several decades later, things are very different. Time has been a healing agent. The area where Sylvia and I grew up is now designated as the Grand Concourse Historic District. It encompasses the area from the Bronx County Courthouse at the south end of Joyce Kilmer Park at 161st Street, north to 167th Street, and stretches east to the Grand Concourse and west to Walton Avenue.

This historic district is once again experiencing gentrification, because of the area's continuing proximity to Manhattan, that borough's very high housing cost, and the fact that many of the apartment houses of the Bronx have been maintained and recently upgraded. The population now of the Grand Concourse, Walton, and Gerard Avenues is a mix of races. Jim, his son and I never felt unsafe there—at least not on a sunny Sunday afternoon. We didn't get a second look as we passed others on the streets.

The area's five synagogues also have undergone transformation: all are now churches. The synagogue named Adath Jeshurun, where for years I went to Hebrew school, is now the Church of God, although it still has Hebrew writing carved on its facade.

Perhaps 20 stores that I remember on 165th Street, less than a half block from the apartment house where I lived, are still open for business—that is, the spaces are still used for stores, but none of them are the same type as they were back in the day. The kosher butcher is gone. The fruit and vegetable store now sells clothing. Tony the shoemaker is no longer in business. Although the merchants are all different, the new iteration of stores is serving the needs of the current community.

As I walked and looked around with Jim and his son that day, I stopped to talk to a cop stationed on the Grand Concourse. He was on duty for a marathon that had been run earlier. I asked him about his precinct and was happy to hear that crime had decreased significantly since the 1980s. He said that we need not be concerned about walking through the neighborhood.

Joyce Kilmer Park has been spruced up with major renovations. The Lorelei Fountain Statue has been repaired beautifully; in fact, the entire installation had been picked up and moved to a new location at the south end of the park. I was amazed to see the city had done that. They'd also created new park entrances and exits.

My friends and I often played in that park as children. In pleasant weather, adults also met there, filling the benches after weekday dinners and on weekends.

In the years 1948 to 1955, at eight p.m. every Tuesday, the park would quickly empty as most everyone went home to watch Milton Berle perform on television's *Texaco Star Theater*. TV was new then, and Uncle Miltie became a pop culture fixture.

As Jim, Russell, and I walked through the park, I remembered that every Christmas season, between Thanksgiving and New Year's Day, the Parks Department erected a tall, blue spruce Christmas tree at one end of the park and decorated it from top to bottom with wooden ornaments and with the obligatory star on top. It was a beautiful sight and I was attracted to it every year. As a Jewish child, I felt it wasn't for me, but I had a classic case of approach/avoidance conflict.

In a similar way, one year during the Passover holiday, my friend Marty and I waved down a cruising Good Humor ice cream truck driver. We were about twelve years old at the time. Marty and I each bought some ice cream, but halfway through gobbling down the treats, we looked at each other and simultaneously realized the ice cream wasn't kosher for Passover. We tossed away the remainder of our ice cream bars, but I was left with an unresolved question of whether the change every year to Passover food was important. That issue remains with me.

I showed my son the school, P.S. 114, which I attended through the sixth grade. Today, the beautiful building still looks modern and clean. It seemed to me to have attributes of an educational oasis, and it revived memories of walking to school, racing home for lunch and then back to school, and finally strolling home at the end of the school day.

I realized how fortunate my neighborhood friends and I were to have gone to this school under the direction of May Hatton. She was a progressive educator who was ahead of her time. I found myself in special classes because of my high IQ test scores, and I had magnificent teachers. There's probably some truth in saying that I learned more in the fifth and sixth grades than in any other schooling. The education I got in that grade school has served me very well for a lifetime.

Sorrell Troskin, my teacher in grades five and six, had a way of letting us teach ourselves, under her attentive guidance. The class was allowed to choose the major topics or units we wanted to learn about, and our teacher integrated that topic into the lessons. For example, when we picked "Housing," it became the springboard for learning history, geography, and mathematics.

One day, Miss Troskin took the class, by bus, to the lower east side of Manhattan to see tenement houses. She did not give us background except to say that this was where immigrants had lived. With a guide from the city, we tromped through a few buildings and were stunned to see the squalor, crowding, and filth, including one bathroom that served several apartments. In silence, the class rode back to our school. It was a powerful lesson.

Between the ages of 9 and 14, Mondays through Thursdays, I went to Adath Jeshurun Hebrew School. I attended Shabbat services on Saturday mornings and Sunday School on Sundays. I wasn't alone; my friends either went to the same religious school or to another one in the neighborhood. The rabbi of our synagogue, Asher Yager, was my teacher.

It was in Hebrew School, when I was nine or ten years old, that I began questioning my religion. One day, when the rabbi was talking about God, I raised my hand and asked, "Rabbi, how do I know that there is a God?"

He didn't hesitate. He said, "Paul, over your lifetime, you'll get many different answers to that question—but in the end, either you believe it or you don't." Though his response was quite progressive for the time, all I could say to him was "Thank you." I said to myself, "If that's the best you can do, you just lost me."

The issue stayed unresolved with me through my entire life until I had a conversation with a rabbi by the name of Max Hausen in the mid-1980s. He was the rabbi of the Main Line Reform Temple in Wynnewood, Pennsylvania. I met him and his wife as they were walking on the boardwalk in Atlantic City.

HIGHLIGHTS OF MY LIFE

I told Rabbi Hausen, "I've never been able to satisfy myself with an answer to the question of whether there is a God."

Without hesitation, he said, "Paul, you're asking the wrong question. You know how to live your life, so do it, and don't worry about the rest."

That lifted the lifelong burden from me.

A Lesson in Miss Troskin's Class

It happened in 1947, when I was almost 11 years old. Eddie, my cousin of the same age, and I were in Miss Troskin's fifth grade class at P.S. 114 in the Bronx. The school, with classes from Kindergarten through sixth grade, was quite wonderful. It was a three-story building on a city block island, standing by itself at 167th Street between Cromwell and Jerome Avenues at the north end of Mullaly Park in the Bronx. It looked and smelled clean. To my eyes, the school always had the look and feel of a new building.

It was an easy walk for me to and from school, through the park and to the apartment at 1020 Walton Avenue at 165th Street. Eddie lived across the street from the school in an apartment house on Cromwell Avenue.

Miss Troskin was not only the best teacher I had at P.S. 114—she was also the finest teacher I ever had throughout all my years of schooling.

On this day in 1947, toward the end of the school year, it was Eddie's turn to give a report to the class. His topic was "Ants." His material was comprehensive, and he presented it in about 15 minutes. Then, as was the style for all reports by students in the class, there was a time for questions and, separately, comments and criticisms. I thought that the report had been excellent because I learned things that were new to me.

On my own, I had been reading about army ants, whose behavior I found fascinating. At the appropriate time in his report that morning, I asked Eddie why he hadn't included anything in his narrative about army ants. I don't recall his answer. The bell rang, signaling the end of the period and time for lunch.

I walked home. Coming into our apartment, I heard my mother on the telephone. She soon finished her conversation and set out the noon meal. She told me that she had gotten a phone call from my Aunt Gus, Eddie's mother, who said Eddie was in tears because he had taken my question as a major criticism of his report. I told my mother that I had asked the question because I thought Eddie's report could have included material about army ants. It is probable that I also thought the report was deficient without mention of those ants, since Eddie had talked about various other ant types. My mother told me that I should not have criticized Eddie because he is "family" and should be protected.

At the time, my mother's explanation made little sense to me. She said no more about it while I ate my sandwich and left to go back to school. Eddie and I didn't say anything about the issue, that day or ever. Yet, the episode stays with me, 70 years later. I wonder if Eddie has any memory of it.

Mr. Solomon's Lesson

Toward the end of E. L. Doctorow's autobiographical novel, *World's Fair*, he writes about his family moving to the Grand Concourse in the Bronx at about 175th Street. Doctorow told of the construction near his new apartment and wrote that it was a new junior high school. I recognized the scene and knew that the building was Wade Junior High School, P.S. 117 (now Joseph H. Wade H.S. 117) on 176th Street and Creston Avenue, a short block off the Concourse.

In June 1948, my cousin Eddie and I graduated from the sixth grade at P.S. 114, where we had been together in the fifth- and sixth-grade classes. That September, we both became students at Wade Junior High School, and we were enrolled together in Mr. Solomon's homeroom class and also in his English class.

My memories of that seventh grade school year are few. It was a pleasant time. I could walk to school and back home along a dozen city blocks of the Grand Concourse. I liked my classmates, who became my new friends.

For the first time, I was in a class with both Jews and Catholics. I found it interesting to debate with a couple of the Catholic boys about the basic tenets of their beliefs. It didn't take very long for me to understand that our discussions would forever yield no change in anyone's views, so the religious talks soon stopped.

Seventh grade was a time of discovery—about girls. It was a new time for me to be surrounded by girls my own age in every class, and to care about it. It was a time of parties with many of the boys and girls from Mr. Solomon's homeroom class.

At the end of the school year in June, all students received report cards with the grades given by each teacher. School work was relatively easy for me, so my grades were all high. My grade in English class was "A." Eddie received the same mark. Knowing Eddie's test scores during the semester, I calculated that his grade should have been lower than mine. I asked Mr. Solomon why our grades were the same.

He said, "When your fathers discuss the report cards, I don't want to be responsible for any hard feelings between the brothers because one son scored higher than the other." I thought then that his logic was flawed. Decades later, I know that Mr. Solomon's job was to teach his students the assigned curriculum and not to make decisions about how grades would be received by his pupils' families. Most interesting to me now is that the episode is one of the few from that year that has stayed with me.

Over the years from then to now, Eddie and I have remained close cousins. He is a skilled, intelligent, and caring man. I admire him and I love him.

The Junior High Championship

Many New York City parks and playgrounds are built with a concrete wall, built specifically for the game of handball—that is, one-wall handball. In most of the USA beyond New York City, the mention of handball evokes an image of the four-wall game, a variety I didn't learn about until well into adulthood.

My father told me that when the great Irish potato famine caused an exodus from Ireland, many of the Irish settled in New York, gravitating toward work in the city's Parks Department. They influenced the Parks Department to build courts for the Irish game of one-wall handball.

In my Bronx neighborhood, there is a fenced-in area, sandwiched between a large playground and a Con Edison electric generating substation, on River Avenue, just south of Yankee Stadium. I learned to play handball there, on its four, one-wall courts. We used no racquets, just our hands, and sometimes wore a tight-fitting leather glove.

Occasionally, the ball used was the pink rubber ball with the brand name "Spalding" imprinted on it. This kind of ball was called a "spaldeen." Other times, the game was played with a small, hard, black rubber ball. The ball was served by one player, who hit it against the wall.

To be in play, the ball had to land over the service line. The other player returned the ball, taking it on a bounce and hitting it against the wall. The players alternated, letting the ball bounce once and returning it to the wall. If the other player did not correctly return the ball, the server won points. If the server missed his shot, the other player became the server. The first player to win 15 points (or sometimes 21) won the game.

This was a game I was good at and one I enjoyed playing. Did I enjoy the game because I usually won, or did I often win because I liked playing?

Outside Wade Jr. High School—where the curriculum for students in the SP (special progress) classes covered grades seven, eight, and nine in two years—there is a large yard. At lunch hour, in good weather, the boys practiced basketball shooting, talked with friends, or played handball on one of the two courts that stood in the yard.

In June 1950, as my junior high school days were coming to an end, I entered a handball tournament sponsored by the school's physical education department. Many boys signed up to play, including my cousin Eddie. The rules were simple: A teacher paired the entrants. The winners stayed on, and the losers were eliminated. After several rounds of play, Eddie and I remained to play in the final match—after our last class, on the last day of school.

Eddie was a good handball player. Our game was close. With the score 16 to 13, Eddie was leading. He had the serve. I returned his serve but then tripped and fell backward, landing flat on my back with a loud thud. My head hit the ground very gently. Eddie turned toward me when he heard the loud sound of my fall. He must have associated the noise of the fall with my head touching the ground.

I got up quickly. I wasn't hurt, and I told Eddie that I was ready to keep playing. Eddie seemed shaken. He didn't win another point. I won the game and the handball championship was mine.

The school year was finished, so Eddie and I left the schoolyard. I never returned and did not pick up the medal for winning.

Some dozen years later, with my school days behind me, I was married with two children and living in the Riverdale section of the Bronx. My neighbor and good friend Jerry S. and I discovered that, on weekends, our contemporaries were using the nearby handball courts to play a derivative of the handball game I'd played as a child. The new game had the same rules, but each player used a short, wooden paddle instead of a bare hand to hit the ball.

Jerry and I experimented and quickly learned that we weren't good enough at "paddle ball" to play with our peers. We decided to go to the handball courts early in the mornings, before others were out and about, to practice with each other. After several weeks of rising with the sun, we increased our skill noticeably and we joined the rest of the guys for competition most weekend mornings. We also learned that the loud sound of the ball coming off the wall and off our paddles early on weekdays was enough to wake our neighbors in the surrounding apartment houses. After that, Jerry and I played at normal hours, to let the neighbors get their full measure of sleep.

Globetrotting

When I think about much of the travel that I have done, I realize that my trips fall into different categories. Some travel was connected with my business; I went to where the clients were. Other journeys were vacations. Sometimes, I found ways to combine business and pleasure travel.

With few exceptions, I did not travel until after college. As a nice Jewish boy from the Bronx, I suppose I lived a rather sheltered life. My parents did travel, most often during the summers when I was at a sleep-away camp. They traveled with their friends to Israel, Europe, and Mexico.

I took one early trip when I was 18 years old. My good friend Alan R., who was a year older, and I talked during the summer about taking a trip to Canada. We had no agenda except the idea of adventure. Mom and Dad agreed and added $100 to my small amount of cash. Al and I said goodbyes to our parents and told them we would come home in two weeks.

We took a bus to Quebec, where we rented a room in the city's downtown, not far from the Chateau Frontenac Hotel. We explored the area with one thing on our minds: finding girls. We discovered that a boardwalk in town near the Saint Lawrence River was a parade area where boys and girls walked back and forth to find companions for the evening. We joined the parade.

After dusk settled into night, we brought our "dates" to our room. It was there that I learned that the nuns had taught the Catholic girls that they would not get into "trouble" if they always "kept their feet on the floor."

One night, we met and fell in with a small group of older men who were circus roustabouts, the workers who raised and lowered the show's tents. They had a beautiful woman with them. She spoke with a French accent that sounded like a cat purring.

After a while, we all went to a local bar and drank a beer or two. Somebody must have made a comment about someone else's mother—or something similar—and a fight broke out between the locals and the roustabouts. Fists flew, as did bottles and chairs. Rather quickly, we heard police car sirens, and everyone headed for the door. Al and I were glad to escape, unhurt and not arrested.

We decided to drive from Quebec into the Laurentian Mountains, which meant we had to buy a car. With our limited cash, that wasn't an easy purchase—yet we found and bought a car for $150. It worked well enough for the week we drove it.

Without a road map, we made our way through the mountain roads that led us from one small town to another. Most had the look of poverty. All these villages had two features in common: an open-air, community oven and a large church. I wondered then if the money to build the church would have been better used on the houses of the town residents.

One night, as daylight vanished, Al pulled our car off the road and parked on some grass. We flipped a coin to see who would sleep where in the car. I lost and curled up as best I could in front with the steering wheel. I was lightly dozing when I heard a familiar sound—the chug-a-chug of a locomotive. I sat up in some panic as I saw the bright light on the front of the engine bearing down on us. Not knowing where we were parked or which way to run, we both stayed put. The freight train passed with a huge *whoosh*. We realized we had parked about ten feet from the railroad track.

We immediately drove to the nearest town, found a boarding house, pounded on the door and—after communicating in "pidgin" French—rented a room for the rest of the night.

Later, back in Quebec, we went from one auto dealer to another to sell our car. One asked us to start the engine and said, "Eet sounds like sheet." We sold the car for $75 and were glad to get that.

In the late 1950s, as I began working as a public accountant, travel became an irregular part of my job. It wasn't unusual to travel to where the clients were located. At that time, many businesses had fled the unions in the New York area and opened non-union shops in the South and West. Often, that is where I traveled to do my public accounting work. My job brought me to places like Florence, South Carolina; McAlester, Oklahoma; and smaller towns like Lake City, South Carolina. This was the segregated South and the segregated West. I saw lifestyles that I had never seen before.

In factories, if the most qualified person to be the foreman was a black man, he might be given the title of foreman but he was told, "Stay in the factory office." A white man would have another title of foreman, and he would walk the plant. If anything needed to be done or changed, the black man would make the decision—but not out on the floor. I saw this several times.

I saw segregated water fountains and segregated bathrooms. For the first time, my shoes received a spit-and-polish shine from a black man.

I was in McAlester, Oklahoma, for the better part of two weeks, and one night I said to a few colleagues, "Let's go to the movies." We looked in the newspaper and found a film that we wanted to see.

PAUL D. NEUWIRTH

We headed to the movie theater. I asked the ticket-taker for four tickets. The lady in the ticket booth hesitated and did not give me the tickets. After a little bit of back and forth, she said, "I think you'll be happier with the theater that's three blocks down the street." It turned out that our group had accidentally chosen the movie theater for blacks, where we weren't wanted. The woman behind the counter was white. Coming from New York, the experience was so foreign to me that I felt like I had been lifted to Mars.

By the late 1950s, I was conscious of segregation on some level, but not its tragic reality—because I'd never brushed up against it. Then, as I traveled the country, I saw segregation on all levels. I saw how the American Indians were treated, and how they lived in shanties. I saw the black field workers picking cotton. I heard, for the first time, black church music on Sunday. For me, this was all eye-opening exposure to the vast discrepancies in our country. My initial naiveté gave way to understanding the reality of inequality in the United States.

As I progressed in the field of public accounting, and as the years went by, I was able to choose work in places where I wanted to go. I traveled across the United States for the work I was doing and hit most of the big cities as I was needed. I also had work opportunities for foreign travel when there were business reasons to go to cities like London or Dublin.

At one point, when I was marketing CPA services, it was part of my job to travel around the United States. For generations, CPAs had prohibited themselves from marketing. That changed when the federal government demanded that the profession eliminate its rules against marketing and solicitation of new business. As director of marketing

HIGHLIGHTS OF MY LIFE

for my accounting firm in New York, I traveled to offices in other cities to talk about marketing and to meet decision-makers of potential clients when I thought there was an opportunity to generate business for my CPA firm.

As a wonderful fiftieth birthday gift, Delaney took me to the Grand Canyon and Monument Valley. I had never been to either place, and visiting both was the fulfillment for me of a long-held dream. Another sensational place that I've been to are the Galapagos Islands, unique for both the species of animals that live there and for the influence on Darwin's theory of evolution. Our visit to the Galapagos was mind-blowing. I hope that this special place in the Pacific, off Ecuador's coast, can preserve its unique quality of visitor respect for its wildlife.

One summer, we went trekking in the Alps. As I think about that, my whole inside lights up with a smile. Our trips to the Galapagos and the Alps were both at the urging of my cousin Eddie, who traveled with us and his mate, Judy.

Being on the Board of Directors of the Medical College of Pennsylvania and its captive insurance company gave me the opportunity to visit Canada's incomparable towns of Banff and Lake Louise. I think Lake Louise may be one of the most beautiful spots on the planet. In my mind, I can picture the engineer-explorers for the Canadian Pacific Railroad discussing where to lay the tracks and where the railroad should build hotels to attract travelers. I imagine them coming around part of a Canadian Rocky mountain to their first view of Lake Louise and being unable to speak because of its incomparable beauty. When again they could talk, they must have said, "This is where the rail line must come." And so, it happened.

The Young Presidents Organization (YPO) is a nationwide group of people who have become president of their companies before the age of

40. Members must leave the YPO after the age of 49. You can imagine that the membership of this group is filled with energy and determination. These are people who want to create and build. As an organization that can generate new clients for a CPA, the YPO is a great group to get in front of. I became a "resource" or regular speaker at their local chapters in and around New York City and, later, Philadelphia.

Because my audience ratings were high, I was asked to speak before regional groups, and then eventually at their national meetings. As I traveled and taught at the YPO, I was dually teaching its members and quietly marketing CPA services for Grant Thornton.

Besides giving my presentations, I was required to be on-call throughout the YPO meeting to answer questions and serve as a mentor. When I wasn't presenting or counseling a member, I listened to all the speakers and participated in all the activities at the YPO conventions. It was a good arrangement for the Young Presidents Organization and it was good for me and my business.

In 1975, I decided that I wanted to see the Olympics in Montreal the next year. I asked my friends in Riverdale if they, too, wanted to go to the Olympic Games.

"Absolutely, yes, count me in," they said.

We would talk about it, and as the time got closer to the opening of the Games, I said, "I've got to send for tickets now. Are you in or not?"

I was surprised when all who had said yes now backed away.

I decided to stay with the plan. My then-wife Bea and son Stephen also had something else to do, so I took Jim and Richard. I had bought a couple of extra tickets, so I asked my mother and father, who were delighted to join us. In our group, the youngest was Richard, at the age of seven; my father was the oldest at 75. It was a marvelous experience for all of us.

HIGHLIGHTS OF MY LIFE

During the week of the games, I think we set an Olympic record for hot dogs consumed and number of bathroom stops.

I had tickets for track and field, water polo, and boxing competitions. I was interested mostly in the track and field events. Jim and Richard fell right into the spirit of the games and were like little adults. They had a wonderful time, too. It was memorable for all of us, including Mom and Dad.

Our sons, Stephen and Jim, each married a Moroccan woman. Both wives grew up in Morocco, went to schools there and in Paris, and met our boys in New York. Nataly and Sandra are wonderful. They and our sons have made beautiful lives with their families.

Jim and Sandra, and her father, Elie Perez, invited Delaney and me to go with them to tour Morocco. Over several weeks, we traveled the country together, starting in Casablanca and moving through the Atlas Mountains and eventually into the south of the country. We saw the highlights of North Africa. Of all the places I've been, the trip to Morocco ranks as one of the most sublime.

I've been to Israel twice. I first went in 1977 as part of a tour group that was run by "Two Ladies from Livingston," New Jersey. Bea and I, with our three sons, planned the trip to celebrate Jim's Bar Mitzvah at Masada in Israel.

Four decades have not dimmed my memories of that special place. Israel is one of the best tourist destinations in the world. There is more to do and see in Israel, no matter what your interests are, than in any other place that I'm aware of.

El Al airlines permitted travelers at that time to couple a trip to Israel with a visit to any city in Europe that was on El Al's routes. Putting the question to my family, Richard said that he voted for Athens. When asked why, he said it was because in school he had studied about the Parthenon. It was a good enough reason, so we added Athens to our itinerary.

When I returned to Israel with Delaney in 1987, I felt a little differently. Perhaps the change in feeling is best explained by a scene as we were walking in Jerusalem on Shabbat. A man wrapped in a tallit was rushing across the intersection of a busy street because he was late to get to the synagogue. I realized at that moment, here was a man wrapped in a tallit, wearing a kippa, crossing an active street, and he was not getting a second look from anyone. He was going to synagogue wrapped in the outward sign of Jewishness and it was okay. Israel is probably the only place in the world where that is possible.

I had no sense of homecoming that so many Jews feel when they visit Israel. It is not my home. America is my home. I am connected to Israel because it is a Jewish state, and because of what it represents and where it comes from. I understand that if Israel were to fall, so likely would Jews around the rest of the world.

Israel is, in some way, a protection of my life—but I am not an Israeli. I think some of the things that the Israelis do are beyond compare. Their medical and other technologies are among the best in the world. Their democracy is a model for much of the world.

But like the USA, Israel is not all superlative. I believe that Israel's ultra-Orthodox lead a life that is morally wrong. But I also think that about any religious group that wants to push its ideas of morality onto others.

Moments in Time

I remember where I was in 1963 when I heard that John Kennedy had been shot and killed. My then-wife Bea and I sat in front of our television set for the better part of the next week, doing nothing but trying to absorb the tragic blow. I realize now that we, like almost everyone in the country, were accommodating to the shock of the president's assassination. In a way, we also were sitting shiva for him and, in part, for what we felt was the passing of an era. As closely as I can remember it, I thought at that time that Kennedy's death was a culmination of creeping lawlessness.

I had first felt the disrespect or disregard for the rule of law when I was in grade school. The school halls had open display cases where students' work could be shown. One day, I saw that sliding glass had been installed in the front of each display case, probably to keep hands out of them. One day afterwards, I saw that the sliding glass panels were locked.

It occurred to me at the time that indifference or contempt for other people's property or work had taken hold. As the years went on, I recognized that more and more lawlessness was afoot in the land—or at least I had become more aware of it.

Certainly there is no relationship between the petty issue of school display cases and the world-changing event of Kennedy's horrific death. Yet at the time, it seemed to me that the president's assassination was a frightful culmination in the straight line of lawlessness. I was wrong. In my mid-twenties, I still carried much of the naiveté of a child. The unhappy circumstances have continued.

What I see from the vantage point of 80 years is that conditions start with the tone at the top. I think our legislators, governors, and judges—those who set the tenor—have let the tone deteriorate. I see also that, as the atmosphere in the political sphere has become accepting of ethical decay, that decay has infected much more of our society.

As I read the daily newspapers and absorb the news from other media, I am disheartened by the tone in the business world. It seems that far too many people are striving to get more money and a higher position as quickly as possible, by any means, irrespective of whether the process is lawful. Unfortunately these conditions appear to be accelerating.

And yet ... as a people, we are able to do so much more and better. Our society put a man on the moon. Think on it: a man on the moon! What a stupendous accomplishment. When we focus on war, senseless murder, theft, corruption, and all the rest of the worst, it is worth remembering the mighty achievement of men walking on the moon. It happened in July 1969, the same time that my Richard was born. To me, both events—although so removed from each other—represent the potential of a glorious future.

When Neil deGrasse Tyson was asked whether he would take the job of Space Czar for the country, he said "No." He declined because our government has decided it is not going to fund the cost of much space exploration. Today, we get to the International Space Station using rocket engines provided by the Russians.

Tyson said that if the will of our people changes and our citizens demand a continuation of space exploration, then Congress will appropriate the money, the president will agree, and our science and ingenuity will renew this worthwhile venture. I look forward to the day when we continue the exploration of space.

A Fall and Its Aftermath

Three years ago, I climbed a ladder to clean the gutters of our house in Gulf Shores. When I came down and reached the last rung, I fell off the ladder and my head hit the concrete driveway, resulting in a concussion.

The potential brain damage of a concussion was severe enough to bring Richard, Steve, and Jim immediately to Gulf Shores. Although it is not unusual in concussion cases, I underwent an almost immediate personality change—one that affected me and had consequences for Delaney. Among other things, I became nasty to all those around me.

At the beginning of this episode, Delaney called 911 and ordered an ambulance to take me to the hospital. I refused to go. In Alabama, if a person says, "I don't want to ride in the ambulance," the first responders cannot force you into the vehicle.

Delaney knew I needed to go to the hospital. Fortunately, Jim quickly came to Gulf Shores on a midnight flight. Very quietly and very effectively, he talked me into going into the hospital. He stayed around to make sure the transition went smoothly.

Stephen talked to a neurologist in New Rochelle and found out about the potential severity of what had happened. He also immediately came to Alabama. When I was in the local hospital, he intervened and stopped my receiving a medicine that would have had disastrous results, potentially turning me into a vegetable. How he knew to do that is a whole different story, but he refused to let that medicine be administered.

Richard also came to help. Steve and Jim were in the midst of doing other things and needed to go back north. Richard stayed with me as I was moved from Sacred Heart Hospital in Pensacola, FL, followed by a rehab facility. Rich stayed with me throughout. He did his work via computer all during that time while he was effective as my "doctor."

He understood what was happening to me and the change in my psychology. He cut to the essence and likely saved me from a series of useless medical tests. At least as important, Richard probably saved my marriage as well, because he stayed with Delaney and helped her to keep her sanity when she was overcome with worry and unable to reason with me.

Then, after several weeks, I was released by the neurologists. I went back to being as close to normal as I ever get. In a crisis, the three brothers knew what they had to do and they did it very effectively. For their various forms of help, I am ever grateful.

The Writing is Completed

At Stephen and Nataly Neuwirth's prompting, this book was written primarily for my family. Those family members closest to me know many of the recollections and stories recounted here. However, it is likely that even those in the circle right next to me may find some new material and some blanks filled in.

Because of their young age, some family members know me only as I am today. It is my hope that this collection of memories will let you know much about how I came to be the person you know.

Although this book is finished, my life's story continues. We will see what new chapters are yet to be lived.

www.ingramcontent.com/pod-product-compliance
Lightning Source LLC
Chambersburg PA
CBHW071735080526
44588CB00013B/2046